S. Patterson

£1

GRAYSON'S WAR

CONTENTS

· DEDICATIONS ·

This book is dedicated to

Everard Farquharson
Slack Alice
Apricot Lil
Dr Tizzard
The Staff at the Cottage Hospital
Maud Shadbolt
Vera Titsall
Freddie Fillet, the Butcher
The Old Gypsy Woman
'Hughie', the Vicar at St Agatha's, 1940–46
The Muffin Man
Fred and Doris, of the Agincourt Tearooms
Faith Gudgeon, Organiste at St Agatha's
Miss Springer, my Ballet Mistress
The Old Lady that Helped Ducks
The Shy Retiring Army Dispatch Rider
Brenda Alcock
Bessie Babcock and the Goat
Everard's Trampoline Instructor
Sterilised Stan, our Milkman
Ada Gringle and her Palm Court Trio
Maud 'Fingers' Moxby, and her Rising Organ
The Nutcrackers' Concert Party
Members of the 'Keep The Stirrup Pump Alive' Association
The 'Railway Buffet Old Comrades Association'
The Bar Staff at the Cock and Trumpet
The Man with the Confused Ferret

. . . and all their many friends who really did help Great Britain through those dark and now distant days of wartime.

Larry Grayson
September 1983

Everard's father and mother just before the safety curtain fell for the last time.

THE FIRST DAY

I shall never forget that Sunday morning of 3rd September 1939. Everard had called around early with some dripping, before going to a wig fitting for his part in *The Maid of the Mountains*, and I had spent most of the morning around at Slack Alice's repairing her rabbit hutch. Then, just before eleven o'clock, I settled down with Slack to listen to the Prime Minister on the wireless.

I can see Slack now. There she was, sitting on her favourite armchair, tin helmet stuck on her head, stirrup pump at her side, a police whistle in one hand and a glass of elderberry wine in the other, as we heard Mr Chamberlain's grave words: 'Therefore a state of war now exists between us.'

There was a silence and then Slack turned to me and said, 'Laz, if I should be taken in this war, there's something I would like you to do for me . . . look after my rabbit.'

'Slack,' I said, 'he'll have carrots every day, but pucker up, they'll never get you, you're indestructible. It's people like you that are the backbone of this country, people like you that grit their teeth and get on with the job, and stand up against all odds. Now then, find your stick and I'll help you back to bed.'

Yes, I remember us going up the stairs and somehow getting wedged at the top, and then all of a sudden the sirens sounded. I think Slack panicked first, but I know we both finished up underneath her bed, and for about five minutes there was fluff everywhere!

Well, after I'd stopped sneezing, and she'd stopped breathing like a carthorse, she looked up at me and said, 'Laz, I haven't moved as quick as that since I used to take my apple water, I must start making it again.'

'Slack,' I said, 'that's the first thing you must do, you owe it to yourself. I remember that photograph you showed me of you dancing around the maypole when you were at school, and who would have thought then that in later years your legs would have started playing you up. I remember Apricot Lil telling me that in your early days you were always the first to get up on the floor at the local hop, and how people used to applaud your fandango. And she said that when you all used to go on those day trips to Clacton, you were always the first to rush down to the sea and get your knees wet. Well, that's what we want to see again when this war's over, so buck yourself up.'

And to give her her due, that's exactly what she did, because as soon as the 'All Clear' sounded I eased her out from underneath the bed, brushed off the fluff and helped her to find her lucky pixie before we made our way downstairs to start on her apple water.

'Come along,' I said, 'a glass a day and you're on your way.' Well, of course, apple water is the easiest thing in the world to make. All you do is take the peel from a pound of apples, place it in a saucepan along with two teaspoonfuls of sugar, the juice from half a lemon and three cupsful of water, then boil for about ten minutes. Mind you, it took Slack about twenty minutes to peel the apples, because her nerves were so bad that not only did she keep dropping them, but she nearly sliced her fingers off twice.

'Slack,' I said, 'for goodness sake let *me* do it or there'll be blood everywhere!' But she wouldn't give in, that's Slack for you!

Well, after that morning she never looked back, and I'm sure it was her apple water that kept her going for most of the war. Sometimes she could hardly lift a leg out of bed, but then she'd reach out for her apple water, and within five minutes she'd be on the move again. She used to swear by it.

Yes, I think Slack would have ground to a halt without it, and to be fair, she did have the worst job in the world for someone with bad legs.

THE GEM CINEMA

You see, for the previous twenty years Slack had been working as an usherette at the Gem Cinema in the middle of town. She was always banging her legs on the backs of the seats and had some terrible scars from the ashtrays. And the job didn't do much for her eyesight either. She said she'd spent so much time in the dark that she felt like a pit pony, and the only time she saw the sun was when they showed a film like *Beau Geste*.

Mind you, her friend Maud Shadbolt was even worse off, because poor old Maud was as fragile as a ha'penny hairnet, and there was nothing of her – if she turned sideways you had a job to see her. She'd been an usherette there ever since the place opened in 1914, and she still didn't know where her feet were leading her! She was alright when she was taking people down to their seats, but she was always tripping over the steps on the way back, and what made it worse was, when the war started, Slack had the brilliant idea of sticking black paper over half the glass on their torches to save the batteries, and it finished up with Maud practically having to crawl back up the aisle on her hands and knees. Anyway, that's when Maud decided to pack it in, which was just as well really, because three weeks later she had to go into hospital to have her knee seen to.

At her farewell party, I remember seeing the surprise on her face when she received her presents. Slack gave her a new ironing board and coal scuttle. Apricot Lil gave her a set of cast-iron saucepans. Bert the projectionist gave her a root from his hawthorn and a roll of nearly new lino, and the manager gave her a special pass for a free seat at the Gem any day except Friday and Saturday. I think Maud was quite overwhelmed.

As for Everard and myself, we bought her one of those large plaster Alsatian dogs, but, unfortunately, before she could thank us she dropped it on her foot. But the presents didn't stop there, because when Maud went into hospital we had another collection, and raised money

GEM CINEMA
SWEETS
SOFT DRINKS
CIGARETTES
TICKET KIOSK
SHOWING NOW
"WILLYS WARTIME WINNER"

to buy her a pair of white crutches so that she could be seen in the blackout.

Sadly they only had black ones, and the day after she came out of hospital she was knocked down by a car – well, if the truth were told, she wasn't exactly knocked down by it, it was parked and she walked straight into the back of it in the dark, but there you are. Anyway, the cottage hospital were quite good, they put her back in the same bed in the same ward, and she felt quite at home. In fact, a couple of the patients didn't even know she'd been gone!

Everard and I visited her the following day, and there she was, lying in bed looking just like Helen Twelvetrees in the film *Panama Flo*.

'Maud,' I said, 'I've never seen you looking so well. I like the new hat.'

'Thank you,' she said, 'it should have more feathers than this, but some dropped off while I was being carried on the stretcher.'

'Well, fancy that,' I said, 'you'd never guess from where I'm standing. Now then, here are some grapes, they should keep you going until they mend your dentures, and try not to swallow the pips. And by the way, Everard here has brought along some white paint to do your crutches. He's already done a white line down the middle of your garden path, so you'll be able to get to your front gate safely, and when we get back he's going to put a ring around your dustbin.'

Well, she was overcome, especially when Everard pulled out his pudding. You see, he'd stayed up into the early hours making it for her as a surprise, and I always remember his voice throbbing with emotion as he said, 'Here you are, Maud, get your gums round that.'

LONDON AMUSEMENTS

Continued from Page TWO.

WYNDHAM'S. Tem. 3028. 8.30. Wed., Th., Sat., 2.30. **COTTAGE TO LET,** by Geoffrey Kerr. Leslie Banks, Alistair Sim, Gillian Lind.

CONTINUOUS REVUE

WINDMILL, Pic-cir. **REVUDEVILLE.** 9th year. 136th Edition (2nd wk.). Cont. 2 to 11 p.m. Doors open 1.30. Last perf. nightly, 8.50.

CINEMAS

CARLTON. **"Choose Your Partner,"** G. Murphy. J. Blondell, Lana Turner (U). **"Bulldog Sees It Through,"** J Buchanan (A).

EMPIRE, Leicester-sq. From 10 a.m **"Northwest Passage,"** Spencer Tracy (A)

Penner in **"The Boys from Syracuse"** (U).

LONDON PAVILION. To-day from 10 a.m. London's two best thrillers. **"Gangs of Chicago"** (A), **"Forgotten Girls"** (A).

MARBLE ARCH PAVILION. Clive Brook, John Clements, **CONVOY** (A); **Saint's Double Trouble** (A); G.B. News. May. 5112

NEW GALLERY. Edgar Wallace's **Case of the Frightened Lady** (A), 12.30, 3.25, 6.20, 9.20. **Grandpa Goes to Town** (U). News.

ODEON, Leic.-sq. (Whi. 6111.) From 11.45. **"Lillian Russell,"** Alice Faye, Don Ameche, Henry Fonda (U). At 1.20, 5.0, and 8.40.

REGAL, Marble A. Mickey Rooney, **Young Tom Edison** (U). 1.8, [illegible], 6.42, 9.29.

STOLL. My Son, My Son! (A). **Bill of Divorcement** (A). Stg. Olive Groves and Geo. Baker.

WARNER. Ger. 3423. Last 4 days of Errol Flynn in **THE SEA HAWK** (A). Progs. 10.0, 2.5, 5.10, 8.10.

CONCERT

QUEEN'S HALL. PROMENADES NIGHTLY at 8. TO-NIGHT, **WAGNER CONCERT.**

ENTERTAINMENT

CHESSINGTON ZOO AND CIRCUS. Daily, 2.30. Wonderful Circus. 3.0 and 5.30. Bus Epsom.

THE BLACKOUT

Yes, I think my grapes and Everard's pudding helped to put Maud back on her feet, and in fact she even got around to writing a poem. It was called 'We Have to Get Used to the Blackout', and it just goes to show the spirit of those early days of the war.

We Have to Get Used to the Blackout

We have to get used to the blackout,
I agree that it's not very nice,
Banged my head on a lamp-post last Wednesday,
And on Thursday I tripped over, twice.

But we've got to get used to the blackout,
It's so Hitler can't see where we are,
I was thinking about that on Friday,
That's the night I was hit by a car.

Now the blackout can make people cheeky,
Take my tip if you have to go out,
If you go, keep your hand on your ha'penny,
There's a lot of strange people about.

Yes, we've got to get used to the blackout,
It's a way of defending these shores,
And I'm doing my bit for the blackout,
'Cos from now on I'm staying indoors!

WINKLE WEEK

Slack was very impressed by Maud's poem, so much so that she took up paper and pen and started to write poetry herself. This is one of the poems that Slack wrote during Winkle Week, 1939.

You Can't Beat a Winkle

Three cheers for British winkles,
They're the finest thing for you,
Three cheers for British winkles,
They will help to see us through.

They're always cheap and cheerful,
And there's lots of them about,
So do your bit for Britain,
Go on, take a winkle out.

They will help us win each battle,
And that's what we all seek,
So let's all pull together now,
And start our Winkle Week.

So come on, grab your winkle,
And attack it with a pin,
And shout our winkle slogan,
'It's better out than in.'

Yes, Slack won a gold-plated winkle-pin for this poem. She also wrote another one called 'Have Faith in a Winkle' but the judges thought it was too religious.

SEEDS
KEEP YOUR END UP
WEEK
DIG FOR VICTORY
RESTAURANT
WARSHIP
WEEK
SHELL
OUT FOR
SHELLS
7
OPEN
HMS
NUTS
HMS
UTS
GIVE
TILL IT
HURTS WEEK

Of course, during the war there were all sorts of 'weeks', Spitfire Week, National Savings Week, Meatless Week, Keep your end up Week, Give till it hurts Week and Warship Week – to name but a few.

I shall never forget Apricot Lil during Warship Week. You see, she'd been getting hot flushes (again!) and she'd been to see Dr Tizzard, and all he'd said was that he couldn't do much for her as it was Nature's way of telling her something, but he didn't say what. All he said was that it might be a good idea if she was to widen her circle of friends, and start taking a cold bath as soon as she got out of bed in the mornings.

Anyway, during Warship Week she wrote off to Portsmouth dockyard to see if she could adopt a sailor for the war, and they wrote back and said it was a kind thought, but at the moment they were only letting ships be adopted, and they didn't think that she would want to adopt a whole ship. Well, she was just about to write back and say she would, when a few of us managed to talk her out of it. You see, we knew what the trouble was. It was all on account of her broken romance with our local butcher, Freddie Fillet. It had all started when she passed his shop one day and saw him laying out his tripe, and soon she developed a crush on him, so much so that every Sunday morning she would cycle around to his shop and roll his faggots. Mind you, this suited Freddie, because she had a wonderful touch and used to do it with her eyes closed. She said it helped her to find any gristly bits. And to be fair she *was* very good, she had the knack of getting them just the right shape and size – she used to weigh them in the palm of her hand – and it was amazing, but you always got three to the pound. But unfortunately they had a row one day. I don't know the ins and outs of it, but rumour has it that he asked her to twist his chipolatas while he rinsed his tripe, and she said she would provided she could keep her gloves on. Anyway, one thing led to another, and she finished up throwing her cycle lamp at him and storming off, so there you are!

Mind you, although Freddie Fillet's chipolatas were legend, Slack could never get on with them, and she used to make her own. She said to me once, 'Laz, I'm like my mother, I like to see what goes in. But of course, now that there's not much meat about, we have to do the best we can. So, I'm going to try a recipe I've been given for utility sausages, and if they turn out alright I'll let you have a few.'

Well, I must say, utility or not, they were delicious so I asked her for the recipe and here it is.

Utility Sausages

8 oz liver
4 oz pork fat
3 oz stale brown bread
3 oz cold potato
1 small onion
salt and pepper
1 teaspoon mixed herbs
1 egg
raspings

Mince the liver, pork fat, brown bread, potato and onion. Then add the salt, pepper, herbs and the egg (save some of the egg to brush over later).

Flour your hands and shape into sausages, then place them into a greased roasting tin. Brush them over with the beaten egg, sprinkle with the raspings, and bake in a hot oven for 30 minutes.

Slack thought they were so tasty that she wrote a little poem, which won her a prize during Save a Sausage Week, November 1939.

Utility Sausages
or
How to Get the Best From Very Little

Who can resist a utility sausage?
Especially now things are so tight.
Who can resist a utility sausage?
Mmm, what a wonderful bite!

I never thought I'd see the day,
When I'd jump out of bed and say,
Who can resist a utility sausage?
Hooray! Hooray! Hooray!

Of course, once Slack takes a liking to something she goes potty, and for the next few weeks it was sausages all the time. Every day she'd rush in with a new recipe for me to try. One day it would be sausages and mock suet balls, then sausage croquettes, then sausage and cheese pie. 'Slack!' I said, 'Slow down, I shall have them coming out of my ears, there's more to life than sausages. A rice pudding wouldn't go amiss, or a rhubarb tart, and I'd give my socks for a chocolate log. But I tell you what, we'll pop around to Everard's, and I'll get him to make us some savoury toast. That's his speciality.'

Well, when we got there, Everard was washing his canary, but he put it straight back in its cage, and within twenty minutes we were all sitting down to a meal to remember.

Yes, if there was one thing that Everard could do well it was savoury toast. In fact when the Vicar first heard about it he was always popping into Everard's kitchen with some excuse – he blessed the cooker five times! And, of course, the word soon spread around St Agatha's, and even further than that. In fact, one Sunday morning he had around a canon, two bishops, eight bellringers, the complete choir, and the first two rows of the stalls. He had more people in his house than there were in church!

And then something dramatic happened. The canon took Everard aside and asked him if he would like to take Holy Orders? Everard said, 'Certainly, how many savoury toasts did you want to order?' Unfortunately, that wasn't quite what the canon had meant, and from that moment on the church seemed to desert poor Everard.

But he still remembers the halcyon days when his name was on every choirboy's lips and they put in a stained glass window over his sink. So do try a savoury toast. And bless you.

Everard's Savoury Toast

a little margarine
3 oz cooked rice
2 peeled tomatoes
1 chopped cooking apple

2 rashers streaky bacon
salt and pepper
a drop of table sauce
4 slices hot buttered toast

Melt the margarine in a pan. Add the rice, sliced tomatoes, and chopped apple, together with the bacon that has been cut into small pieces.

Fry lightly until the bacon has been cooked, then add the sauce and the seasoning and spread on to the toast.

Wind up the gramophone and put on the record of the Temple Church Choir singing 'Oh for the Wings of a Dove' and serve while hot.

Spreading the good word during 'Have a Fishy Week'.

CHRISTMAS 1939

Then came the first Christmas of the war. I remember quite clearly calling round to see Slack on Christmas morning, and how proud she was of her new air-raid shelter that the council had just put in her garden.

'Come and have a look inside,' she said, 'I'm going to make it home from home, a little nest where I can rest.'

Well, I stuck my head in, and pulled it straight out again! 'Slack!' I said, holding my nose, 'I'm sure there's been cats down there . . . either that or one of the workmen's left his socks. You can't sleep in that atmosphere, light a joss stick or something. You'll never be able to give the Vicar his cucumber sandwiches down there!'

'Laz,' she said, 'that is the honest smell of mother earth, good old British soil, and I might as well get used to it, because one day they're going to lower me down into it anyway.'

'Slack,' I said, 'you do have a wonderful attitude, You were exactly the same when you were knocked off your bicycle by that laundry van. You just picked yourself up and said, "It's just as well my drawers weren't starched" and carried on. Yes, you always manage to make a joke of everything – even when Maud had her knee seen to, you managed to make her smile when you called her Hopalong Cassidy.'

Well, I think Slack was a bit overcome by what I'd said, because I remember her brushing away a tear on her apron as she offered me a mince tart and a glass of Vimto. But before long she was her old self again, and we settled down to our traditional Christmas morning game of draughts – best out of three, and the loser pulls the chicken. No prizes for guessing who used to pull the chicken with most regularity!

You see, even with a war on we managed to hold on to tradition. For instance, every Boxing morning we would all stroll around to Everard's, where we were each given mince pies, a glass of punch and an invitation to try his lucky dip. Mind you, I was always the unlucky one and usually finished up with hair grips or a sink plunger, but it was the spirit of the thing that mattered, and that was the same with Slack's Happy New Year pudding too.

You see, every New Year's morning we would pop round to her place for a taste; it was like a ritual. She would ply us with elderberry wine until we started singing, then she would rush in from the kitchen, put the pudding on the table and rush out again, and she would only reappear if there was applause and cries of 'Luv'ly grub'. This was because one year Everard swallowed two threepenny bits, a St Christopher and a tapwasher, and Slack was always a bit apprehensive after that.

Slack's Happy New Year Pudding

4 oz flour
4 oz breadcrumbs
4 oz suet
4 oz raisins
4 oz currants
2 tablespoons treacle
½ pint milk
1 teaspoon baking powder

Mix the ingredients well. Put into a greased basin and cover with greased paper. Boil for about 3–4 hours.

— BLANCHE HACKETT —

Now, as soon as the New Year celebrations were over, came that first week of January, and what a bleak week! I remember I was standing in the wool shop, trying to make up my mind whether to knit myself a long vest with a flap, or go the whole hog and knit myself an all-in-one bodywarmer with a mandarin collar and kneepads, when who should walk in but Blanche Hackett.

'Blanche!' I cried, 'I haven't seen you since the Harvest Festival at St Agatha's, when you fell against the font and grabbed the Vicar's surplice.'

'No,' she said, 'I've been in hospital again having my seventh baby, and that's seven in six years, I feel as if I'm never off my back.'

'I don't know how you do it, Blanche,' I said. 'Washing all those nappies out in this weather, it must play havoc with your hands. I only have to rinse through a couple of teatowels and my hands are raw.'

'I don't mind that so much,' she said, 'but my nerves are all in shreds, I only have to hear a bedspring creak and I come out in a cold sweat.'

'Come along, Blanche,' I said. 'What you need is a tonic; something to buck you up, have you ever tried a portion of savoury meat custard? Everard swears by it, he got the recipe from his grandmother in the country; it was found in her apron pocket the day after she fell down the well. The ink had run a bit, but he could still read it. I'll get a copy from him after Evensong, and pop it through your letterbox.'

'Lawrence, that sounds ideal,' she said, ''cos the last thing I want at the moment is something heavy lying on my stomach.'

Well, I got a copy of the recipe for Blanche, and I made a copy for myself . . . here it is.

Granny's Savoury Meat Custard

4 oz cold meat
2 eggs
½ pint milk
chopped parsley
salt and pepper
tomato purée

Put the meat through the mincer twice.

Beat the eggs, add the milk, and then add the meat and parsley, salt and pepper.

Put into a greased basin and steam gently until set, then turn out and serve with the tomato purée.

A few weeks later I met Blanche again and, do you know, she was looking so much better. 'Blanche,' I said, 'you're a changed woman.'

'Yes,' she said, 'and I've made a big decision, I'm not having any more children until this war is over. I've told Bert that if he wants to do something useful, then he can join the Local Defence Volunteers, they're looking for people with pent-up energy, so let them have the benefit from now on.'

'Good for you, Blanche,' I said. 'Start as you mean to carry on. You've done your bit for Britain, now leave it to the others, put your slippers on and give your legs a rest, and don't forget to take your iron tablets. Besides, your Bert will enjoy it in the L.D.V. There's not many of them at the moment, and they've only got one rifle between them, but he can always start with a broom handle and work his way up from there, and it's probably for the best anyway, because the person who was in charge of the rifle last week shot himself in the foot, and you don't want all that do you?

'Mind you, your Bert will have to be quick, because there's a lot of people thinking of joining. In fact, Slack Alice's neighbour has just joined, Mr Belvedere. You remember him, he used to be the local insurance man, the one who always looked as if he had about a week to live. Anyway, Slack says that he's changed a lot since he retired, and apart from standing at the bottom of the garden talking to himself, he's turned into quite a nice person. I know he was always getting on Slack's nerves complaining about her rhubarb spreading and coming up through his floorboards, but Slack says he's changed for the better and was one of the first to offer help when she had trouble with her overflow recently. He knew exactly where to find her stopcock, and she'd been looking for it for years. Slack thinks it's the war that's changed him, because her rhubarb still comes up through his floorboards, but instead of complaining he now makes loads of rhubarb tarts, and is forever passing them over the fence. She says she's sick to death of rhubarb tarts, but doesn't like to offend, especially after his wife left him because of a row over a rice pudding.

'Anyway, a week last Tuesday, Slack sat down and wrote a poem about Mr Belvedere, and how he had joined the L.D.V. And it was published in the local paper last week. Unfortunately it was put under the obituary column by mistake so you may have missed it. It was called "A Tribute to a Neighbour" by Alice Clackett.'

THE L.D.V.s GET THEIR STRIPES

BADGES of rank are to be worn by the L.D.V., which has now been organised to cope with possible future expansion.

The basic unit is the section consisting of approximately 25 men under a section commander. Although local circumstances may cause variations four sections form a platoon, four platoons a company, and four companies a battalion, which, therefore, is normally about 1,600 men.

L.D.V.s are Now Home Guard

MR. CHURCHILL'S suggestion in his last broadcast that L.D.V.s should be called the Home Guard has been officially adopted.

Mr. Eden, Secretary for War, announced in the Commons yesterday that it was proposed to submit an Order in Council to the King giving the L.D.V.

A Tribute to a Neighbour

Three cheers for Mr Belvedere,
He's joined the L.D.V.,
He couldn't join the Army,
He's got water on the knee.

But he's standing up for Britain,
With good old British grit,
'Tho I don't suppose he'll run about,
I should think they'll let him sit.

But it's men like him that volunteer,
And heed our nation's call,
He'll be out there in the forefront
With his dodgy knee an' all.

So three cheers for Mr Belvedere,
I've had water on my *knee,*
If he's stuck outside this winter,
Then rather him than me!

Madge Hawthorne, winner of the 'Crack the Vicar's Walnuts' competition in aid of church funds. August 1940.

Vera Titsall's 'cousin' defusing some of Slack Alice's elderberry wine.

A steel sentry box, 1941. Slack Alice applied for one of these as a replacement for her outside toilet which was blown up early in the war. She's still waiting to hear.

A VISIT FROM EVERARD

I remember that winter well. One cold day I was lying on my palliasse, thinking 'I wonder if Eskimos ever do risk a quick dip, or is there too much danger of icicles?' Then suddenly I heard a knock on my knocker. 'Heavens!' I thought, 'who can it be? It can't be the Vicar again, I've already put my hand in my pocket for him, and it can't be the Muffin Man or I would have heard his bell. It must be Everard.' And sure enough it was. I opened the front door and there he was, frozen stiff, standing on one leg, looking like a stork that has lost its way and flown straight into a brick wall.

'Everard,' I said, 'you look like the "Missing Link". Come in and get something hot inside you or you'll never get to see another summer. Sit down and I'll get you something hot from the pot, you can't keep going through a winter's day on three yeast tablets and a ginger biscuit. Here, have a dollop of this, it'll help to keep the brass monkeys away.'

Well, the colour soon came flooding back into his cheeks. 'Everard,' I said, 'whatever brought you out on a day like this? You know you have a weak chest, and Dr Tizzard would go spare if he knew, especially as he promised your woodwork teacher he would look after you. He's bent over backwards for you, and this is how you reward him.'

Anyway, we sat down and I found out what it was all about. Apparently, Everard's canary had caught a chill, and he had called around to see if I would lend him my Mickey Mouse hot-water bottle to put on top of the cage at night. And how could I refuse? Well, Everard couldn't thank me enough when I gave it to him, and in a voice choking with emotion he said, 'That's what friends are for.' Then he turned and with a brave smile opened the door and walked out straight into a ten-foot snowdrift. And as he disappeared, I thought to myself, 'Thank goodness he had some of my brass monkey soup.'

Brass Monkey Soup

2 potatoes
3 carrots
4 sticks celery
few leaves cabbage
2 onions
1 turnip

1½ oz margarine
salt and pepper
2 quarts stock
1 oz flour
a little milk

Wash the vegetables, and then chop them finely.

Melt the margarine in a pan. Add the vegetables, and fry lightly for about 5 minutes. Add the seasoning and stock, and allow to simmer for about 2 hours.

Then, blend the flour with a little milk. Stir into the soup and cook for a further 10 minutes.

Of course, Slack used to make her own soup during the winter months too, but she used to get carried away with it all, and all you could taste was garlic and chilli powder. When she opened her front door the smell of it used to blow your hat off, but that's Slack!

MEAT FOR ALL AT CHRISTMAS

THERE will be enough meat for all at Christmas—if the Ministry of Food can overcome the transport difficulties.

The Ministry have every hope. Road and rail transport workers and dockers are joining in the great December rush to see that the Christmas joint is on the table.

Their job, difficult enough in the black-out, is made harder by the fact that large quantities of imported meat have to be hauled long distances because of the smaller supplies of home-killed meat.

Day Without

There is a temporary shortage of meat in some districts.

Sunderland, for instance, will have a meatless day to-day.

HAVE A MEATLESS WEEK

Of course, at various times during the war we were urged to try and have Meatless Weeks. This was alright for some people, but to others a week without meat could be a very long week indeed, especially if they were used to having it regularly.

But Slack knew all about meatless weeks because she'd even had them in peacetime, and so she put pen to paper once more, and wrote one of her most rousing poems of the war.

Have a Meatless Week

Some people have it twice a week,
And then again on Sunday,
And if there's some left over,
Then they warm it up on Monday.

But what we need are meatless weeks,
To build up our reserves,
And not the old excuses
Like, I need it for my nerves.

I know some people crave for it,
Of that I have no doubt,
But even in the good old days,
I often went without.

So, come on, have a meatless week,
And help us win the war,
And when you get your next 'best end'
You'll enjoy it even more.

Mind you, there was one person who wasn't all that impressed, and that was Ethel Braithwaite – or 'Big Ethel', as we used to call her.

I saw her outside the Post Office that week, and I could tell she wasn't in the best of moods.

'Ethel,' I said, 'I haven't seen you since you popped around to borrow my curling tongs, not that I'm in a hurry for them, but how are you?'

'Well,' she said, 'things aren't going too well at home at the moment, and it's all to do with this meat business. You see, my Bert works hard all the week, and the one thing he looks forward to on a Sunday is his bit of belly. Not that I'm all that bothered myself because I'm easy either way. And whereas Bert likes a lot of meat in the middle, I'm quite happy with just a touch around the edges.'

'Ethel,' I said, 'we've all got to cut our cloth according to our whatsits now that there's a war on, so why not try a meat substitute like nutty faggots and rice?'

'No,' she said. 'Rice is alright for blowing you out, but half an hour later you're hungry again, and that wouldn't be any good for me because I've just started working nights at the rubber factory, and eight at night until six in the morning is a long stretch.'

'Well,' I said, 'I am surprised. The last time I saw you, you were working in that meat pudding factory with your mother, and I remember how proud she was when the works manager gave you that diploma for your gravy. Please give her my regards when you see her, and tell her she must come around and read my tealeaves again when she's free. Meanwhile, keep pulling away at your new job, and every time I see an elastic band I shall think of you.'

Now, there were lots of people like Ethel whose husbands looked forward to something a bit special on a Sunday, but of course, with meat being short, people's thoughts turned more to fish, and in fact we had our first Fishy Week in 1940.

That was the week that Everard and I were due to go cockling together down at the coast. But now there was barbed wire around all our favourite places, and you could only cockle if you were local, or had a friend in a good position. So, we stayed put, and I started off Fishy Week by making a patriotic fish pie, with rough puff pastry. Now, if there's one thing I love getting my teeth into, it's rough puff. If I had my way it would be rough puff all the time. In fact, during the war when meat was short, people started putting rough puff around everything – well, almost everything – and what better than fish?

Patriotic Fish Pie

6 oz cooked white fish
seasoning
3 tablespoons tomato sauce
1 tablespoon breadcrumbs
1 teaspoon chopped parsley
8 oz rough puff pastry
1 beaten egg

Flake the fish, and mix with the seasoning, sauce, breadcrumbs, and chopped parsley.

Roll the pastry into an oblong shape, then cover the middle third of the pastry with the mixture. Fold the pastry over into an envelope shape, press the edges together, and brush over with beaten egg.

Bake in a hot oven for 20 minutes, then reduce the heat and bake for a further 15 minutes. Serve hot or cold, and stick a Union Jack on top if you want, and why not?

STICKS TO BEAT THE INVADER

STOUT ash staves 5ft. to 6ft. long will be the "arms" of the Fitness Force which now goes on parade without fear of arrest for "unlawful drilling."

The sticks will be provided by the Central Council for Recreative Physical Training. They are *not* broomsticks—and the War Office would rather we didn't call the volunteers for spare-time military drill a "Broomstick Army.

The lifting of the 1819 ban on this sort of training was hailed yesterday by demands for training facilities in every town and village in the country.

In Every Town

They are to get them. The C.C.R.P.T., which five weeks ago began to promote centres for pre-military fitness training, plans to add rapidly to the 180 already established.

DOT FAIRBRIGHT

Where would we have been without our fish pies? But of course, some people had to go one better, like Dot Fairbright – and she was all swank and no drawers. She would never admit to having a fuller figure, although everything she wore looked as if she'd been poured into it, and that was like trying to get a quart into a pint pot! But what was strange was that, winter and summer, she always wore red wellingtons and her fox fur – and that always looked as if the dog had had a fight with it the night before!

I remember being behind her in the fishmonger's during Fishy Week, and when it came to her turn to be served, she said in a loud voice. 'Oh, I think I'll have some nice haddock again today, as I'm entertaining someone from the council this afternoon.' Which I suppose was true in a way, because they sent someone around to look at her guttering. Mind you, all he got was a cup of tea and a rock cake, and he had to practically kiss her boots to get that!

This is one of Dot's recipes.

Haddock de Poshe (What else?)

1 fresh haddock
8 oz sausagemeat
breadcrumbs
seasoning
2 oz margarine

Wash the fish. Make a slit down the centre, and then stuff with the sausagemeat.

Place the fish on greased paper in your baking tin, sprinkle with breadcrumbs and seasoning, then put little pats of margarine on top.

Cover with greased paper, and bake in a moderate oven for about 45 minutes.

Yes, Dot Fairbright always felt she was a cut above the rest, but Slack had her well taped. I remember Slack saying to me once, 'You can always tell what people are like by looking at the washing on the line.'

I'm still trying to work that one out. But that was Slack, very down to earth, as she showed in her patriotic poem, 'Herrings'.

Herrings

A lovely fish is a herring,
When it's done in a nice casserole.
It mixes quite well with tomatoes,
And between them they fill a big hole.

I love it, it's cheap and it's cheerful,
And there's plenty of it in the sea.
Plus, Hitler can't blockade a herring,
So I feel that that's one up to me.

So, get out your frying pans, ladies,
And whether a herring or sprat,
We'll turn round and say to old Hitler,
Up your pipe! Pick the bones out of that!

There were certainly no airs and graces about Slack, especially when she lost her rag, and she really hated Hitler. She said once, 'Give me five minutes alone with him and my crimping shears, and I'll do what they did to Napoleon!' Yes, it never paid to get on the wrong side of Slack.

But most of the time Slack was as soft as putty. I met her outside the Co-op one morning, and she was all red-eyed. 'Slack!' I said, 'Whatever is the matter?'

She wiped away a tear and said, 'It's Bert, our projectionist at the Gem, he's been called up.'

'Never!' I said, 'He's far too old for the army!'

'No,' she said. 'He's been called "upstairs". He dropped dead yesterday on his way to work, and the film we're showing all this week keeps reminding me of him, it's called *They Died with their Boots on.*'

'Never mind, Slack,' I said. 'Last week you were showing *Halfway to Heaven* and it must have been an omen because now he's up there. But at least he's left his mark. Remember all the fun the audience used to have when he got confused, and used to show John Payne and Maureen O'Hara paddling along in a canoe upside down, and Charlie Chan walking in backwards looking for clues? That's what gave a bit of novelty to the Gem, and people never had to sit through a boring murder mystery. He usually managed to show the last reel somewhere in the middle, and at least people didn't have to wait for the last bus, sometimes they were out of the cinema by nine o'clock. Now then, pucker up and come back with me. I'll make you a nice cup of beef tea.'

'No thank you,' she said, 'I'm going home to bake a special pudding in his honour, and all the staff are going to have some when we have two minutes' silence before we take the ice-cream around.'

And here is the recipe that Slack made up herself on that very sad occasion – we'll meet again pudding. She even used her last egg in it, but that was Slack. At moments like that she'd give you the laces out of her boots.

We'll Meet Again Pudding

2 oz margarine
2 oz sugar
1 egg
½ teacup milk
4 oz flour
pinch bicarbonate of soda
2 tablespoons raspberry jam

Cream the margarine and sugar. Add the egg and milk. Beat well together, then stir the mixed flour and soda. Last of all add the jam.

Bake in a greased pie dish for 30 minutes, turn it out and sprinkle with sugar.

Cheapest Cinema Seat May be 5d.

The price for the cheapest cinema seat is to be raised from 3d. to 5d.

This is one of the recommendations made by a branch of the Cinematograph Exhibitors' Association to members in its area extending from Clitheroe in the North to Macclesfield in the South.

Old prices of admission were 3d., 4d., 6d., 9d., 1s., 1s. 3d., and 1s. 6d., and the proposed new prices are 5d., 8d., 10d., 1s. 2d., 1s. 6d., and 1s. 9d.

The increases are due to higher overhead charges and the new entertainment and purchase taxes.

B.B.C. Music at Work to Go On

The B.B.C.'s "Music While You Work" programmes are having such a tonic effect on the spirits and productivity of war workers that they are to be continued beyond the short term for which they were first planned.

Managers and directors of firms have written to the B.B.C. thanking them for the "ginger" which the music helps to put into the working of the employees.

FIREWATCHING

It was a sad day that, but Slack realised that life had to go on, especially as the staff had to do their spot of firewatching on the roof, although how Slack ever managed to climb up there with her legs I shall never know! But she did, and she was up there twice a week with her stirrup pump and dustbin lid, and she didn't give a fig for anything.

She'd take up a bottle of her homemade wine, five blankets and two hot-water bottles, and she was ready for anything. Then, about four in the morning she would pop into the little hut that was up there, and fry herself a couple of firewatcher's fishcakes.

One Sunday morning, she came around with some for me to try. 'Here,' she said, 'have a nibble at these.' Well, I've nibbled a few things in my time, but nothing as worth while as a firewatcher's fishcake; we shall never see their like again.

Firewatcher's Fishcakes

6 oz cooked fish
1 lb mashed potatoes
a little white sauce
1 tablespoon chopped parsley
salt and pepper
1 egg
breadcrumbs

Flake the fish. Mix with the potatoes, sauce and parsley, salt and pepper, and the mixture should become stiff. If not, add a little beaten egg or a few breadcrumbs until you get it right.

Then coat with egg and breadcrumbs and fry.

Yes, Slack certainly showed her true colours during her fire-watching nights, and I think that Maud would have been proud to have been at her side. The only trouble with Maud was she had enough trouble staying awake during the day, let alone all night! In fact I don't think I've ever met anyone as weary as Maud – except Everard when he has one of his turns – but I've even seen Maud fall asleep stirring custard!

But she used to have a wonderful excuse. She used to say, 'Well, Winston Churchill has little naps all the time.' I used to say, 'Yes, but not while he's stirring custard!'

Anyway, one day she said to me, 'I've found the answer. Cheese pudding, that's what I've been needing, and it's certainly done the trick; you're looking at a new woman.'

'Maud,' I said, 'what can I say? I'm thrilled for you. I wonder if you could give me the recipe, Everard could do with a bit of a boost.'

Well, it took me two and a half hours to write down the recipe. Not that it was long, but I had to keep waking her up!

Maud's Cheese Pudding
(for the weary)

1 small onion
6 slices bread and butter
1 egg
a little made-up mustard
salt and pepper
$\frac{1}{2}$ pint milk
$\frac{1}{2}$ pint water
4 oz cheese
1 oz breadcrumbs

Boil the onion until it is tender, then chop finely. Cut the slices of bread and butter into pieces and arrange in a greased pie dish.

Break the egg into a basin, and add the seasoning,

milk and water and chopped onion. Beat well, and add three-quarters of the cheese.

Pour over the bread and butter, and allow to soak for about 30 minutes. Mix the remaining cheese with the breadcrumbs, and sprinkle over the pudding. Bake in a moderate oven until set.

Maud had to save up her cheese ration for this recipe, and sometimes she had to use margarine instead of butter, but she was happy, and that's the main thing, because she heard a couple of weeks later that she had to go into hospital again to have her other knee seen to, and all she said was 'I don't know why they bother to give you knees if you can't keep them working properly. Next time I'm going to ask for ones that swivel.' Now how can you beat a spirit like that?

THE OLD GYPSY WOMAN

It was about this time that I was due to go on tour with my Strolling Players, and we were going to perform two wonderful plays – *To Have and To Hold* on Mondays, Tuesdays and Wednesdays and *She Only Reached the Edge of the Bed* on Thursdays, Fridays and Saturdays. Unfortunately, during rehearsal I touched on an old nerve and overstretched myself, and the next thing I knew I was in the cottage hospital with my leg up. I remember Dr Tizzard calling to see me, and how he clutched my hand as he told me that I would never play croquet again.

But, one had to make the best of it, and I remember lying there one rainy afternoon – I had just finished reading the *War Cry* and was waiting for Everard to bring in the *Young Soldier* – when suddenly my thoughts turned to those halcyon days before the war.

I recalled one summer's day in particular, when I was wandering hither and thither looking for a four-leafed clover and hoping my luck would change. Then, suddenly, an old gypsy woman appeared as if from nowhere, and I recalled her very first words to me: 'Hallo dearie, how are you off for clothes-pegs?'

Well, we struck up a conversation, and soon I found myself sitting next to her campfire toying with a bowl of gypsy casserole. I was so overcome that I agreed to buy three dozen pegs, and she was so overcome she started to tell me my fortune by saying: 'You have a too trusting nature, never turn your back on anyone. . . . But your biggest attribute is you have a wonderful memory . . . yes, a wonderful memory.'

I thanked her for everything, and walked slowly away deep in thought at what she had told me. Then suddenly, something hit me on the back of the neck – it was a large turnip. I turned, and there was the gypsy woman smiling benignly. 'You forgot to pay for the pegs,' she said.

Well, over the years I've lost all the pegs, but I've never lost her recipe for gypsy casserole and here it is.

Gypsy Casserole

3 turnips
$1\frac{1}{2}$ oz margarine or goose fat
2 carrots
8 oz peas
salt and pepper
breadcrumbs
a little milk

Cook the turnips in boiling salt water, then drain well and mash with margarine. Then, dice your carrots and do the same, and then mix them with the peas.

Grease a casserole dish, and place a layer of turnips in the bottom, followed by a layer of peas and carrots, and continue the process. Lastly, put a few pats of margarine on top, plus a few breadcrumbs, and a little milk.

Put the lid on the casserole and place in a moderate oven for about 15 minutes.

— THE GARDEN FÊTE —

Yes, all this, and many other things came flooding back as I lay in that hospital bed. But soon I was on the mend, and I remember the day I came out. It was a Saturday, and there was Everard waiting for me with the tandem.

'Come along,' he said, 'we're going to the garden fête at St Agatha's.'

'I can't ride on that tandem,' I said. 'I've had my leg up for ten days, it'll set me right back if my legs go too fast too soon. I don't mind coasting but can you stand the strain?'

Well, he was all heart. He pedalled all the way and I just dangled. Hey ho, up hill and down dale. What a gay day! How Everard kept going I shall never know, but eventually we arrived and eager hands welcomed us. The first thing they did was to ease Everard off the tandem and take him to the first-aid tent for oxygen, then we made our way slowly around the stalls and sideshows.

I remember seeing Vera Titsall there – looking like Mae West. She was selling kisses at sixpence a time, and loving every minute of it. Every hour too, for that matter.

'Vera,' I said. 'Steady on, you'll have yourself in a swoon the way you're going on.'

'Well,' she said, 'there's nothing to stop me now that I'm divorced, so why shouldn't I spread a bit of pleasure, especially as it's all in a good cause. Plus, you never know, I might find a new friend.'

'Yes,' I said, 'but the way you're going at it you'll finish up with all your teeth loose.'

'Well,' she said, 'they want more than a peck for sixpence, and who am I to disappoint them?'

Mind you, she soon changed her tune when she had to lie down for half an hour after a big naval stoker had put down a pound note and practically eaten her alive, but she was always game was Vera.

Then there was Slack, of course. She was doing very well looking after the coconut shies, until a wooden ball bounced back and hit her straight between the eyes. After that she didn't know whether it was St Swithin's Day, the Cup Final or Pancake Tuesday!

But the most successful stall was called 'Dip your finger in and tell me what it is'. Now, this was run by good old Dora Dabbs, and she was ninety if she was a day, but she still turned out with her mystery dip. Actually it was a tapioca pudding with caraway seeds, and the idea was, you paid your money, then they blindfolded you, and you had to dip your finger in, taste, and guess what it was.

Well, the guesses ranged from rabbit broth to cocoa, but there was one winner, Mr Wellbeloved, or as he was known locally, 'the verger on the verge'. He was eighty-one years old, and had been engaged to Agnes Springle for the last thirty. I remember her saying to me once, 'There's nothing wrong with him, he just needs a bit of a push.'

'Agnes,' I said, 'if he leaves it much longer he'll need more than a push, they'll have to carry him into church!'

Anyway, he won the dip. And Dora said afterwards that she thought the reason he guessed it first time was that he'd always been a bit deaf. I've been trying to work that out ever since!

Yes, they were good days. But then came the dark days when many people spent every night down in their air-raid shelters. I remember Slack getting ready to go down, and she had so much stuff with her I thought she was moving. Even the rabbit was worried!

'Slack!' I said, 'you don't need all that down there. I can understand the four crates of elderberry wine and the eight dozen candles, but what on earth do you need with nine blankets, five pillows, three eiderdowns, two pairs of wellington boots, three hot-water bottles and your banjo? I know you like a good strum, but you'll never be able to play it down there, and you know you go out of tune if the damp gets to your G-string!'

She said, 'Ah, but Bert Postleswaite takes his accordion down the shelter with him, so what do you say to that?'

'Yes,' I said, 'but he takes up less room than you, he's only got one arm, and he can't play it at the moment anyway, because his wife's ricked her back and she's the only one that can pump his bellows.'

At least Slack had the decency to raise an eyebrow at that.

But it was no good trying to tell her. Then one night she dropped her teeth on the floor and spent all night trying to find them. After that she had a good clearout.

But it's just as well she kept going down the shelter, because one night a bomb fell right on her outside toilet. As Slack said, she could have been sitting there one moment, and knocking on the Pearly Gates with her drawers round her ankles the next!

And of course, Slack had to write a poem about it, didn't she?

BEFORE, DURING AND AFTER THE RAID – No. 1

HEALTH HINTS FOR SHELTER NIGHTS

— and the help that is ready if your home is hit

For your own and the country's good you should know (1) how best to live a healthy and comfortable shelter life, (2) the help you will get if you are bombed. Read the information given below, and the leaflets which you will shortly receive.

TO AVOID INFECTION

Illness spreads more quickly when people are crowded together. So make all members of the family gargle before they start for the shelter. Any of the usual gargles will do; a

Bedding should be aired daily. It is even more important for the shelter than in your own home. The daily airing will keep the bedding sweet and fresh, and *will help to get rid of dampness.*

They've Bombed our Outside Toilet

They've bombed our outside toilet,
It happened in the night,
I was sleeping in the shelter,
And it gave me quite a fright.

I heard a sort of whistling,
Like the bombs make when they fall,
Then the ground shook all around me,
And the noise was something cruel.

When I looked out of the shelter,
All I saw was lots of dust,
Then I recognised our cistern,
I could tell it by the rust.

Then I saw a bit of S-bend,
And half the toilet seat,
And found the chain and ballcock,
On a lamp-post down the street.

Yes they've bombed our outside toilet,
And they've razed it to the ground,
But they've saved our council money,
It was due to be knocked down.

– NATIONAL DOUGHNUT – WEEK

Anyway, I don't know whether it was delayed shock or what it was, but a few days later Slack developed a terrible craving for bread pudding, and she had it for breakfast, dinner and tea. In fact she even took some down into the shelter in case she felt a bit peckish during the night. Well, I could see what was happening to her, she was beginning to bulge.

'Slack,' I said, 'you've never been a small woman and you've always liked your food, but with all that bread pudding you're eating, one night you're going to squeeze into that shelter and we'll never get you out! Your bunk bed has already collapsed twice, and your varicose veins are like the main roads on a map. Think about the customers at the Gem. Who's going to lead them down the aisle if your legs pack it in? They still haven't found a replacement for Maud, so at the moment your two legs are doing the work of four, and you told me yourself that when you take the ice-cream tray around you keep getting a touch of the vapours, and I'm not surprised! So come along, sort yourself out. You've got a lot of years in front of you, and you won't get very far if you have to spend the rest of your life wearing surgical stockings.'

'Laz,' she said, 'it's easier said than done, and *you* must have had a craving at sometime or the other.'

'Yes,' I said, 'for spotted dick, but I got over it, and so can you. Listen, Slack, next week is National Doughnut Week so why not give up your pudding and dunk a doughnut instead? Everard has started dunking his already, so why not join the throng? Also, you'll be able to write one of your wonderful poems about it, because they're holding a competition, and the first prize is a week for two in Harrogate, and you'll be able to take the waters. You could take Apricot Lil with you, and you could put your name down for a mud-pack – you've been promising yourself one for years. Come on, Slack, you can do it.' Well, eventually she took my advice, and here is her poem:

Doughnuts

When you're in your air-raid shelter,
And you're feeling rather blue,
Be a devil, dunk your doughnuts,
Just like other people do.

You can dunk them into cocoa,
You can dunk them into tea,
I dunk mine into my custard,
Every day at half-past three.

You can dunk them into gravy,
Into soup or even stew,
You can dunk them into anything,
It's entirely up to you.

Let us not become downhearted,
In this land of lib-er-ty,
For it's time to dunk our doughnuts,
All together – one – two – three!

Unfortunately she didn't win first prize, that was won by Madge Perkins from the Co-op who wrote a very strange poem called 'I Can See a Whole New World through the Hole in my Doughnut'. I couldn't make head nor tail of it, but the Mayoress liked it so there you are! It takes all sorts.

Mind you, it did get Slack over her craving and that was the main thing, because I remember the agonies Everard went through when he craved, and he must have been one of the worst! You see, he once had a craving for brandy snaps, and if he couldn't have one he was like a bear with a sore behind. Yes, I've known him to lie awake all night thinking of brandy snaps, and in fact sometimes he used to break out in a cold sweat.

But then I introduced him to liquorice allsorts, and he had his first good sleep for years. Yes, he never looked back after that, and he's never been able to thank me enough. In fact, he can pass a brandy snap now and not blink an eyelid. And for those of you who can also control your emotions, here's the recipe for those very brandy snaps.

Brandy Snaps

4 oz treacle
2 oz margarine
4 oz sugar
4 oz flour
½ teaspoon ginger

Warm the treacle and the margarine, then mix thoroughly with the other ingredients.

Put teaspoonsful on to hot baking tin a few inches apart. Bake in a hot oven for about 5 minutes, and roll around the handle of a wooden spoon while still hot.

Yes, even our Vicar had cravings in a way. I remember him saying to me one wet afternoon – while we were cleaning out the font – 'Lawrence, why is it that when I visit anywhere, I am always offered the same old thing . . . egg and cress sandwiches? I can't remember the last time I was offered a honey rusk or a piece of guardsmen's cake. What a sad world we now live in.'

Well, he was such a dear old gentleman, and I could see that he was near to tears, so I rushed home for my cookery book and gave him this recipe.

He passed away on the following Friday.

Guardsmen's Cake

8 oz shortcrust pastry	4 oz margarine
8 oz currants	4 oz sugar
8 oz flour	2 oz lemon peel
½ teaspoon bicarbonate of soda	1 egg
½ teaspoon grated nutmeg	a little milk

Lightly grease a medium-sized cake tin, and roll out the pastry. Cut out a piece to fit bottom of tin and place it inside. Roll the remainder of the pastry, and place it around sides of tin.

Wash and drain the currants. Sieve the flour with the soda and nutmeg, then rub in the margarine and add the sugar, currants and peel. Whisk the egg in a little milk, and add it to the ingredients.

Put the filling into the baking tin, and bake for about 1½ hours. When you first put it in, your oven should be hotter than is usual for fruit cakes, and you should turn down the heat slightly after about 15 minutes.

Yes, it was a very sad day when our Vicar was taken from us, especially as we had just started up a fund to refurbish his weathercock, but life had to go on, and I remember the day that our new Vicar arrived – he fell over twice getting out of the removal van!

Vera Titsall turned to me and said, 'He doesn't look as if he's got the strength to pull the curtains let alone the bell!'

'Vera,' I said, 'looks can be deceiving. Take Everard for instance, look how many times the old Vicar asked him around to pull the big one. The secret is not how you pull it, but knowing when to let go. Anyway, Everard's always had a knack when it comes to campanology. He started off with handbells and worked his way up, and I'm sure if he's asked nicely he'll show the new Vicar the ropes.'

Well, of course, that's exactly what happened, and within a week the new Vicar was pulling away all on his own. The only trouble was, everything sounded like 'The Bluebells of Scotland' with a touch of the hiccups, but in the event it didn't matter, because the following week came the invasion scare, and although we were winning the Battle of Britain all church bells were ordered to remain silent and only to be rung as a signal that the invasion had started. And of course the last thing that people wanted to hear during that late summer were the bells.

That Wednesday afternoon I went around to Slack's to pull her parsnips, and she said to me, 'Laz, if those bells start to ring, I don't know what I shall do. I heard the Muffin Man coming down the street this morning, and when *he* rang his bell I nearly wet myself! And he's only got a little one!'

'Slack,' I said. 'Not to worry. Sit down and write a poem. Put all your fears down on paper, and they won't seem half as bad. Get it off your chest, you know you always feel better when you do that.'

Well, this is the poem she wrote in that late summer of 1940. When she'd finished it, she went to bed with a bottle of port, and we didn't see her for two days.

Invasion Bells Muddle

MORE confusion has arisen over the ringing of church bells.

The War Office told a *Daily Mail* reporter last night:—

"There is only one rule about the ringing of church bells—and that is when parachutists are in the immediate vicinity."

Yet, according to the September issue of the Lincoln Diocesan Leaflet, the general officer commanding the troops in Lincolnshire has issued instructions to all vicars that the bells will be rung for two purposes.

The leaflet says: "In the event of an imminent or attempted invasion a 'general alarm' will be rung by the sounding of every bell in every church throughout the county (perhaps indeed throughout England) as a tocsin.

Five-minutes Peals

"The bells will be rung loudly and confidently as a call to battle —the peals continuing for five minutes continuously.

"In the case of a 'local alarm' necessitated by the descent of enemy parachutists or air-borne troops one bell will be tolled at short intervals of a few seconds in the church nearest the occurrence.

"It is preferred by the authorities that the incumbent should supply the bell-ringer, and only if this is not possible should a soldier ring the bells."

Slack Alice was very moved when she saw this photograph of a splendid old gentleman of the Home Guard. She said it reminded her of her grandfather who fell off the top of a flagpole during the Lord Mayor's Show in 1911.

Members of Mr Belvedere's Home Guard Company – Bill Ben and Wee Ed.

Here I am making a quick call to Everard to remind him to put his dustbin out.

We Don't Want the Vicar to Pull It

We don't want the Vicar to pull it,
It's the last thing that we want to hear.
He's pulled it before, and he'll pull it again,
But not till he get's the 'All Clear'.

The end of his rope can get knotted,
A left-handed reefknot is best,
He should tie something thick round his clanger,
Like a scarf or a thick woollen vest.

Yes, we know that our Vicar is nervous,
And we hope that the Germans won't land,
If they do he'll be holding his trousers,
And pulling the bell with one hand.

So let's hope that there's no need to pull it,
And the Home Guard can rest on their pikes,
Then he'll get the 'All Clear', and without any fear,
He can pull it as much as he likes!

COCKLE COVE

Yes, those were restless days and restless nights. One night I was lying awake, toying with a walnut whirl and thinking, 'if they do invade, I wonder if they'll land at dear old Cockle Cove?'

Then my mind went back to those carefree days before the war, when Everard and myself used to cockle there. But the clearest memory of all was my very last visit. You see, Everard had just gone down with a touch of the mumps, plus he was due to have his ears pierced, so I decided to go down and cockle on my own.

Well, somehow the place didn't seem the same, especially as they were just about to knock down the Agincourt Tearooms, and what a bitter blow that was for all of us who over the years had come to love their Cockle Cove pudding. But of course the owners – Fred and Doris – were now in the twilight of their lives, and it was getting darker by the minute.

I well remember walking in there for the very last time. A pile of broken tables and chairs were over in one corner, and there were floorboards missing, where dry rot had taken its toll. The kitchen looked as if it had been hit by an earthquake, and the windows seemed as if they had been rattled to death by a typhoon.

But there was Fred, carefully taking down the photographs from the walls. There was one of the King's visit in 1902, plus the Thrashabouts Concert Party, 1914, and a posed photograph of the local fire brigade taken on the day that the chip-pan caught fire in 1921.

I had to turn away, and as I did I saw Doris sitting there on top of a pile of rubble, silently knitting a balaclava for the cat – it hated the cold – and for once I couldn't think of a thing to say.

It was Doris who broke the silence, and I remember her words to this very day. She looked up at me and said, 'Sorry . . . we're closed.'

It was people like Fred and Doris who made our seaside resorts what they were, with such mouthwatering dishes as Cockle Cove pudding.

This is how we made it.

Cockle Cove Pudding

1 tin plums
8 tablespoons cake crumbs
just under 1 oz custard powder
½ pint milk
a little sugar

Strain the syrup from the fruit. Then heat the syrup, and when it's nearly at the boil, pour it on to the cake crumbs.

Place the plums in the bottom of a pie dish, add the cake crumbs, then blend the custard powder with a little of the cold milk. Boil the remainder of the milk, add a little sugar and then pour on to the blended custard.

Return the mixture to the saucepan, and simmer for about 5 minutes, then pour it on to the fruit, and bake in a moderate oven for about 15 minutes.

Yes, dear old Cockle Cove. But of course the invasion never came, because Hitler decided that it might not be such a good idea after all and how right he was! Soon we were thinking about Christmas. I remember Christmas morning I went around to Slack's to blow up her balloons – again! Then we had our usual game of draughts before moving off to Apricot Lil's for a slice of honey sandwich cake and a glass of her parsnip wine. Then Everard invited everyone around to his place where he served cheese straws and a touch of his red ruby, before surprising us all by coming in from the kitchen carrying a tray of little fruity cakes.

'Everard,' I said, 'when you whipped off your doily I had the surprise of my life! I didn't know you had it in you, I was expecting plum duff. What a gay day! You've been hiding your whisk under a bushel, get out into the world and make your mark. I'll have a word with my good friend Crispin Touche and see if he can get you a position under the head chef at the Queen's Hotel. But meanwhile let's all form a chain and celebrate down at the Happy Bullock. We'll have one or two in there, then we can move on to the Bunch o' Plums and the Friend in Hand, before finishing up in the Cock and Trumpet for the loyal toast. They've got Faith Gudgeon on the piano this morning, so we can sing 'Land of Hope and Glory', then have a silver collection to buy her a new hearing aid. 'Come along,' I said, 'all form a chain behind Slack, and we'll conga down to the Bullock, and don't go too fast or you'll trample her to death.'

Well, we all arrived in one piece, and the festivities began. Slack was drinking egg-flip and cider. Lil was drinking rum and barley wine. Maud started with a bottle of Guinness and a Manhattan cocktail, and Everard went mad with a snowball. As for myself, I had a small port and a packet of crisps and kept my eye on the others. Not that it made any difference, because by the time we reached the Cock and Trumpet, Slack had steam coming out of her ears, Lil was crying, Maud had to be carried in and propped up against the piano, and Everard had lost all the feeling in his left leg.

There they all were, looking like the walking wounded, but they did all manage to stand for 'Land of Hope and Glory', which Faith Gudgeon just about mangled her way through before banging out the last chord and falling off of the piano stool. Yes, a Christmas lunchtime to remember. I don't think Maud remembered much, because the last I saw of her, they were lifting her into the back of the baker's cart – even the horse was surprised! But she got home safely and that's what matters most. As for Slack, I had to see her home, and that was like trying to steer a blancmange in a fog. How I ever managed to get her through her front door I shall never know if I live to be twenty-eight! But she bounced back, and on Boxing morning she was out in the garden watering her rhubarb as usual. Good old Slack! As for Everard, I went around next day to make him a bread poultice and finished up doing a morning's baking! But I didn't mind, because it gave me a chance to jot down his recipe for little fruity cakes, and here it is.

Try one, it could change your whole life!

Little Fruity Cakes

3 oz margarine	salt
3 oz brown sugar	1 cup sour milk
1 egg	3 oz sultanas
8 oz flour	2 oz cut orange peel
1 teaspoon bicarbonate of soda	almonds
1 teaspoon mixed spice	

Cream the margarine and sugar, and beat in the egg. Mix the flour, soda, spice, and a pinch of salt, then add them with the sour milk, the sultanas and peel.

Then half fill some small paper cups with the mixture, and put a split almond in the centre of each one.

Bake in a moderate oven for 15–20 minutes.

LAST DAYS FOR CREAM BUNS

ICED cakes, cream buns, éclairs, and fancy biscuits are to go—for your safety.

Last night came five items of news each telling of some new measure designed to prepare Britain against siege, strengthen our coast defences, and put the country generally into readiness to meet invasion.

The news was of :—

—CREAM BUNS

AFTER August 5 it will be an offence for bakers to place "sugar" on any cake, biscuit, bun, pastry, scone, bread, or roll after baking.

But between August 5 and September 2 you can buy these tit-bits if your retailer has them. During that period the baker will use up his icing-sugar reserves.

After September 2 the selling or buying of confectionery of this kind is forbidden.

"Sugar" includes glucose and fondant but not chocolate-icing.

September 2 is also the last day for the manufacture of candied peel and crystallised cherries. Drained or cut peel and glacé cherries may, however, continue to be manufactured.

Brides Save Sugar to Ice the Cake

THERE will be no more iced wedding cakes made by the confectioners after August 5, when the Ministry of Food ban on icing comes into force.

Sales of iced cakes, if they are of the kind which keep, will be allowed until September 2.

"Where wedding cakes are concerned," a Ministry of Food official said yesterday, "we are back at the same situation as in the last war.

"If a bride wants an iced cake she will have to save up her sugar ration for the icing."

— EVERARD'S TWINKLE —

Well, we were soon into January 1941, and how the weeks dragged along. I remember it clearly because Everard had still been having trouble with his left leg, and Dr Tizzard had told him that he needed to spend more time out in the fresh air, and if possible to get a job with a bit of bending, as the backs of his legs needed tightening up.

So, Everard took on a job with the council, painting white lines in the middle of the road. I remember seeing him one frosty afternoon in the middle of the road, paint brush in hand, bending over in a ballet position. Then as I walked up behind him I saw something twinkle at me. 'Everard,' I said, 'what a funny place to put a cat's-eye! Whose idea was it to stitch it on to the seat of your trousers?'

He said, 'Well, I'm afraid of being knocked down in the dusk, I've already had two near misses, at least now they can see me.'

'Yes,' I said, 'but you can't go into the Friend in Hand with that stuck on your trousers.'

'Why not indeed?' he said. 'It's a talking point. I'm thinking of having one sewn on the front too, it's only like wearing big sequins.'

'Everard,' I said, 'I shall never understand you if I wait from now until my lettuce comes up. Sometimes you're shyness itself, then all of a sudden you seem to welcome the pointed finger. Come along, put your brush away, I've been keeping something in the oven for you all the afternoon, sweetbreads with peas and forcemeat balls.'

Well, I've never seen anyone move so quickly, and within fifteen minutes he was sitting in front of my fire using his fork like a steam-shovel.

'Everard,' I said, 'slow down, there's peas all over the carpet. Nobody is going to take it away from you, in fact there's second helpings, so try to eat with a bit more decorum. You were never like this when we used to have afternoon tea at the Gingham Tea rooms. It used to take you fifteen minutes to nibble through a teacake and a drop scone . . . now you're acting as if the world's going to end tomorrow.'

But of course it was my own fault, I should never have made such a tempting dish for such a cold day, and let me tell you it's not a dish for toying with. In fact even I have had to control myself when it's been put in front of me. So why not try it? You can even stick some parsley on your forcemeat balls and make a wish . . . I do.

Sweetbreads with Peas and Forcemeat Balls

12 oz chilled lamb's sweetbreads
1 small carrot
1 onion
1 teaspoon chopped parsley
pinch thyme
pinch ground cloves
½ pint water
1 tablespoon cornflour
few drops browning
small tin peas

Wash the sweetbreads in salt water, then scald and throw water away. Add the carrot and onion along with the parsley, thyme, cloves and ½ pint of water, and simmer for about an hour.

Strain the gravy and thicken with the cornflour and a little browning. Then heat your peas, and keep your sweetbreads hot in the gravy while you're frying the forcemeat balls.

Arrange the sweetbreads on a hot dish, surround them with the peas, and place your forcemeat balls on top.

For the forcemeat balls you need:

4 oz breadcrumbs
2 oz vegetable fat
½ teaspoon mixed herbs
1 egg
salt and pepper
raspings

Mix breadcrumbs, fat, herbs and egg together, season, then form into balls and roll in brown raspings. Fry until golden brown.

— THE KEEP-FIT CLASS —

Now, get something like that inside you and you'll feel as fit as a fiddle. It did wonders for Everard; he could suddenly paint twice as fast. In fact he finished painting the white lines so quickly he put himself out of work for a fortnight! But he didn't mope about, and one of the first things he did was to go and see his old scoutmaster and book the scouts' hut every Sunday morning for keep-fit classes.

'Lawrence,' he said, 'I'm going to keep it up, and I want everyone to join me, young or old. We need to keep our bodies fit for what lies ahead, and I can see the errors of my ways.'

'Everard,' I said, 'I've been trying to drill it into you for years. A healthy body makes a healthy mind, so think big, get Slack Alice to join, and Vera Titsall, but forget about Maud until you get on to handstands. Start them all off by standing on one leg for five minutes and see how you go, forget about press-ups until later, because once Slack gets down on the floor you'll never get her up. Don't try to push too far too soon, give them a fighting chance. I'll mention it to Slack, I'm going round there today to brush the greenfly off her leeks. Leave it to me.'

Well, when I told her, Slack was quite taken aback. 'Me?' she said, 'I don't think I'm fit enough for all that.'

'Slack,' I said, 'that's the whole idea! Once you start sticking your chest out and doing your deep breathing exercises, your whole body will be flushed and you'll feel a tingling in places that you didn't know could tingle. You'll finish up galloping down the aisle at the Gem, and you'll be climbing up to do your firewatching like a monkey after his nuts. You've got nothing to lose and everything to gain. Think of it, in a few weeks' time you'll be able to get your knees under your chin, and that could open up a whole new life for you. Imagine the thrill of being able to carry your own coal in, instead of having to ask Mr Belvedere. He'll be delighted as well.'

'Laz,' she said, 'you're quite right. I've let myself go over the years,

Alice Clackett
Mafeking Ward
The Cottage Hospital
Tuesday

Dear Laz

As you will see, I am in hospital again. This time I am in traction and strung up in a very strange way. My right leg is connected to my left arm by overhead pulleys and my left leg is connected to my right arm by overhead pulleys, which means that it's a bit difficult to write this letter, because every time I put my left leg down, my right arm shoots up in the air and I lose my pen. I have tried writing on my side, but if I do I usually finish up with my left arm between my legs and my right leg around the back of my neck.

In fact, last night I went to scratch myself and did a complete somersault, and I think I've put myself back about three weeks.

Mind you, the woman in the next bed is worse off than I am, because although she's strung up the same as me, she's on a water bed, and she only has to sneeze and she's up and down like a yo-yo. The worst thing is meal times, though. Every time her knife slips the air is full of peas and carrots, to say nothing of gravy, and at lunchtime today the woman in the opposite bed only looked up for a second and a pork sausage hit her straight between the eyes! We had rice pudding yesterday, and half of it is still up on the ceiling! So, mustn't grumble I suppose, there's always people worse off than ourselves.

All for now
Love
Alice

P.S. They are just coming round with Lancashire Hotpot, I'm putting my umbrella up!!

and I realise now that I should have kept my bicycle. I only sold it because I was too lazy to soap the saddle.'

'Slack,' I said, 'stop blaming yourself and start again. Stick out your chest and remember you're British.'

Well, that's exactly what she did, and she even wrote a poem about it called 'Stick it Out for Britain'.

HOME GUARD WILL BE 'ALL FIT' FORCE

THE Home Guard is to be a thoroughly fit force. It will lose many of its "old timers." Officers will be younger.

A survey has begun with the object of weeding out all men who may not have the endurance needed to meet a large-scale invasion attempt.

All Home Guards are concerned in this revision, whether local commanders or rankers.

Neither past experience in the Services, social position, nor any consideration except physical fitness will affect decisions.

Many retired officers are in the Home Guard ranks as well as men who served in two or three wars. For them age alone will not be a bar. Many men at 60 are physically fit.

Fitness Dictator Urged

M.P. Weds at 62

Stick it Out for Britain

Stick out your chest for Great Britain,
Let's put on a big bold front.
Let's show them what we're made of,
How we'll stand and bear the brunt.

Stick out your chest for Great Britain,
Till you nearly burst your bra,
But stop if you start going dizzy,
You don't want to push it too far.

But we all need to show we're uplifted,
So throw out that bra if it's slack,
Then go out and buy a size smaller,
And do it up tight at the back.

Yes, let's stick out our chests for Great Britain,
And let's kill two birds with one stone.
Make it one in the eye for old Hitler,
And two for our troops here back home.

Unfortunately, the keep-fit class became a bit accident prone and it only lasted for about three weeks. Everard became a bit over-confident and finished up landing awkwardly on the wooden horse. He lost his voice for three days, but it didn't affect him all that much because it also sent him deaf. And then there was Apricot Lil, she hit herself over the head with some Indian clubs and started getting double vision. And poor old Maud was hit on the nose by a punchbag and fell over the rowing machine, and she'd only popped in to watch! And then Faith Gudgeon dropped the tea-urn on Vera Titsall's foot, and then did her back in trying to lift it on to the draining board in the kitchen, and Slack got completely carried away, tried to do the 'scissors' and somehow jack-knifed and finished up under the ping-pong table.

Well, Dr Tizzard syringed Everard's ears and ordered complete rest and no spices. Apricot Lil completely lost her nerve when it came to crossing the road, because with her double vision she was seeing twice as much traffic coming and going, and Faith Gudgeon went off tea and started drinking cocoa instead. Vera Titsall borrowed Maud's crutches for a week, and poor old Slack finished up in what had almost become her second home – the cottage hospital.

In fact, over the years, she had spent so much time in there they were thinking of naming a ward after her, but it never came to anything.

Still, give Slack her due, she went in without a moan, despite the fact that she couldn't get her legs together, and the first thing she did was to write to her friends. I've always kept her letter, because it just shows the spirit of those times.

Read it and be thankful.

Yes, Slack certainly knew how to grin and bear it. I remember going to see her in the cottage hospital on the Friday, and there she was, all bound up and all strung up – looking like something out of *The Mummy's Curse* – but still managing to play a game of draughts with one of the nurses.

'Slack,' I said, 'what a novelty. That's the first time I've ever seen anyone pushing the draughts with their nose. We'll have to play it that way next Christmas. It will make a nice change, and next time I come in to see you I'll bring some billard chalk, to stop your nose from skidding.'

'Laz,' she said, 'I hope to be out before you come in, but if you come in before I come out, then there's a little something I'd like you to do for me.'

'Slack,' I said, 'when you've stopped talking backwards I'll make a note of it.'

'Well,' she said, 'there's one thing I've missed while I've been in here, and that's a nice marconi and tomato savoury, so if you come in before I come out, will you bring me one in?'

'Slack,' I said, 'I've told you a hundred times, it's not marconi, it's macaroni. Marconi was the man who sent the very first message across the Atlantic.'

'No,' she said, 'you can't fool me, it was Macaroni who did that, and he was a Scotsman. Anyway, there's some marconi in my cupboard in the kitchen, and you'll find all the other bits and bobs in the pantry. I've left the back-door key in a jam-jar out in the shed, but be careful when you go in there because I don't want you to wake up my tortoise, he's hibernating.'

'Slack,' I said, 'that's all he seems to do. I'm sure there's something wrong with him. I've seen the shell, but I haven't seen him stick his head out for the last three years. Are you sure he's still in there?'

'Yes,' she said. 'Last Christmas I saw him stretching one of his back legs – I think it was one of his back legs!'

'Well,' I said, 'all I can think of is that he's decided to sleep through the war. He must take after Everard. But not to worry, I'll make you a special savoury at my house, and the day you come out of hospital you can be my guest.'

Well, that's exactly what happened, and I can see her now, sitting at my kitchen table, balanced on five cushions, and savouring every mouthful. She was cock-a-hoop, and so will you be when you try it. Go on, be bold.

Macaroni and Tomato Savoury

4 oz macaroni
2 onions
1 oz margarine
1 tin tomato purée
mixed herbs
chopped parsley
salt and pepper
hard-boiled egg (optional)

Boil the macaroni in salted water until soft. Then drain and pour cold water over it to stop it sticking together. Then fry the sliced onions in a little margarine.

Mix the macaroni, tomato, seasoning, parsley, and the fried onions together in a pan, and add the remainder of the margarine, and stir all together until thoroughly hot again.

If you want, you can chop up a hard-boiled egg and sprinkle it over the top.

I sprinkled two eggs over mine, but that was as a special treat for Slack.

But Slack still had to take it easy for a while, and so Apricot Lil stood in for her at the Gem. Lil still had a slight touch of double vision, and often showed a single person to a double seat, but her eyes eventually got back together, and once she was able to see the screen in focus she quite enjoyed it. What's more, she took a real shine to Percy, the new projectionist.

I remember seeing her at the shops one morning, and she looked a different person. 'Lil,' I said, 'it's the first time I've ever seen you out shopping without your curlers in. You'll have all the shopkeepers on their knees, they'll think you've come into money.'

'Well,' she said, 'I'm meeting a gentleman friend, and we're going to choose a ring.'

'Lil,' I said, 'You mean you're about to get engaged? I'm thrilled for you.'

'No,' she said, 'a gas ring. Percy may be moving into my spare room, and he likes to wash his own socks.'

'Lil,' I said, 'that's what you've always needed, a companion, someone to make the house feel lived in. I know the agony of lying there alone thinking. "If there were only someone in the house to share a mug of Ovaltine and a wafer biscuit." Good for you, Lil, this could be the start of something big and it's doing wonders for your spots already. Dr Tizzard will be over the moon.'

'Yes,' she said. 'My Percy's very easy to get on with, and he does like my cooking. We had savoury sheep's tongues the other day, and he said he'd never tasted anything quite like them. He really likes simple food like rissoles, but the only trouble is, I'm a bit worried about making some because of what happened to my mother and father. You see, she made my father rissoles for breakfast every day, and every day he would sit down and eat them, then go and do an eight-hour shift at the gasworks. Then, one Sunday morning, he came down, ate his rissoles, then without so much as a word, got up slowly from the table, put his cap on, and walked out of the front door, and we never saw him again.'

'Lil,' I said, 'don't torture yourself, I have a recipe for rissoles at home that will make Percy's tastebuds jump for joy. I'll give it to you, but you can tell him it's your very own and it can be our little secret. What's more, next week is National Rissole Week so you can kill two birds with one stone, because the whole nation will be sitting down to them.'

Here is that very same recipe which I like to think brought them closer together.

Ragamuffin Rissoles

3 oz cold minced meat
1 egg
½ tablespoon made mustard
salt and pepper
1 lb mashed potato
a little flour
dripping

Add the meat, beaten egg and seasoning to the mashed potato, then blend it into a paste.

Shape into cakes on a floured board, then fry them in hot dripping. Remove, drain, give them a dollop of your favourite sauce, and the taste will stick in your mind forever.

And here is the poem that Slack wrote all those years ago, called 'Rally Round a Rissole'.

Apricot Lil's father who suddenly disappeared on 7 July 1942 after eating his 4,328th rissole.

Rally Round a Rissole

Let's rally round a rissole
During National Rissole Week.
Just think of British rissoles,
And give yourself a treat.

If you've flogged yourself for Britain,
And you've just got in from work,
What better than a rissole?
To provide that extra perk.

It's one way of beating Hitler,
They don't have them over there,
For a rissole's truly British
And it's made with loving care.

So rally round a rissole,
Have them every day this week,
Raise your frying pans for Britain,
And let's hear your rissoles squeak.

Slack sat up all one night to write this. But she couldn't sleep anyway, because she'd had some rissoles for her tea, and they'd given her terrible heartburn.

– THE CONCERT PARTY –

Mind you, Everad missed National Rissole Week completely, he was still in bed! He said he was still suffering from the accident, and that his toes hadn't straightened out properly. He just used to lie there and doze. Honestly, the times I knocked his knocker! Even the Vicar couldn't get him to rise, and that was one of the reasons he was asked to give up his position in the choir.

As I said to him, 'Everard, your rendering of "Ye Holy Angels Bright" may have been in demand ten years ago, but the world has moved on, and you can't live on a legend. You're lucky they've kept your position open as organ pumper for Miss Gudgeon, and that's only because you were kind to her cat after it had been run over by that steamroller. Come along, pull yourself together. If you really can't get out of bed, then at least do something useful while you're in it. Why don't you try to finish off that scarf you were knitting for your friend in the Merchant Navy? It'll go nicely with his earmuffs. Or write to your friend Basil to see if there's any vacancies yet in the Nutcrackers' Concert Party. He promised to put in a good word for you, and you always got on well with his mother. Remind him about the days when you had a week together with the Flash in the Pans at Gorleston. You went down very big there with your Indian rope trick, if you remember. In fact, you did it so convincingly you went down with malaria on the Wednesday.'

Well, eventually he got around to writing the letter, and a week later received a reply. Yes, there was a vacancy as long as he didn't mind dressing up – and that was never a problem! Yes, they were about to start their new season with an engagement in the local park. This time it was Spanish Onion Week, and I can see Everard's face now, and how flushed he was that he had been chosen to play the part of Carmen Miranda in a number called 'Flash Fiesta'.

I well remember the first time he showed me his castanets. 'Olé,' he cried, as he clicked them together.

'Everard,' I said, 'I know you're rhythmic, and I know you love chilli con carne, but you'll *never* be able to play the part of Carmen Miranda. You can't even walk in those built-up shoes, let alone dance! And another thing, what are you going to stick on your head? You know that bananas are like gold dust around here these days.'

But he wouldn't be told, so there he was on the day – looking the image of his mother – all dressed up with three pomegranates on his head, plus a wax banana borrowed from Maud Shadbolt's fruit bowl.

Well, he managed to stagger through one chorus of 'Ay Ay Ay Ay Ay I like you very much'. Then he was suddenly struck by cramp. Well, I never want to hear a man scream like that again.

'Everard,' I said, 'you frightened those twelve people in the audience to death! It even gave me a nasty turn. Now then, take off those silly shoes, put your mac over your dress, and we'll go back home on the bus.'

Well, I hadn't told him but I'd got something ready for him as a surprise. It was my very own castanet casserole. And it's a funny thing, but now every time he gets cramp it's the first thing he asks for.

Castanet Casserole

3 oz rice
2 Spanish onions
1 tin tomatoes
1 bayleaf
6 peppercorns
3 cloves
½ teaspoon granulated sugar
salt and pepper

Cook the rice in boiling salted water until tender, then drain. Fry the sliced onions, then add the rest of the ingredients and simmer for about 15 minutes.

Remove the bayleaf, cloves, and peppercorns, then add the rice. Turn into a greased casserole dish, and bake in a moderate oven for about 30 minutes.

Of course, Everard was most disappointed that he'd failed to make an impact as Carmen Miranda, but he was livid when he heard that Thelma Shackle was taking over the part. And not only that, but she was also doing her Alice Faye impression, singing 'San Francisco'. And what annoyed him most was that he'd secretly been practising the very same number with Faith Gudgeon on the piano, and had spent hours in front of the mirror trying to capture Alice Faye's smile.

'Everard,' I said, 'stop tearing yourself to pieces. Why don't you form your own concert party? You could go all over the place with it. You could entertain the workers in the factories during their lunch hours, and send them back to work rejoicing, you could be on everyone's lips. You could always get Faith Gudgeon on piano, and you've got that friend who does a bit of sword-swallowing and fire-eating. He should be out of hospital soon, he's already got his voice back, and they're taking the bandages off next Wednesday. Then there's the Hilda Titchburn Young ladies, and they're always good for a bit of tap dancing. I know they're not as young as they used to be, but I'm sure they'll squeeze into their tap shoes for a good cause, and providing the music isn't too fast they should be good for three minutes at both ends, and somewhere in the middle you can do your Alice Faye *and* your Marlene Dietrich. Start off with "Falling in Love Again", then do your favourite, "See What the Boys in the Backroom Will Have". You could open up a whole new career for yourself, and think how proud your mother and father would have been of you. Their whole life was spent in the theatre, and they would have been there to this day if that safety curtain hadn't fallen on them while your mother was balancing on your father's shoulders. Wasn't it funny how your father was always saying "Your mother is gradually driving me into the ground!" but at least at the very end they were inseparable.'

But of course Everard wouldn't take my advice – as usual. 'Lawrence,' he said, 'you know me, I like to feel my way before I jump into anything.'

'Yes,' I said, 'but that's the story of your life, and you've had so many opportunities. I know you had problems when you played Peter Pan and they flew you in on the wire upside down, and that time you played Aladdin, when the spout dropped off your magic lamp; but you mustn't look upon life as one big disaster. The world won't wait for you forever, get out there and show them what you've got.'

But it was no good talking to him, and I had other fish to fry. 'Everard,' I said, 'I shall be going away on tour next week, and I'm leaving you a special recipe to buck your ideas up. It's called get up and go mould, and for goodness sake make some. The recipe will make enough for four or five people, so spread it around a bit. Give some to Slack, or whoever else looks a bit down in the dumps, and I want no excuses.'

And this is the recipe I gave him.

Get Up and Go Mould

3 lb spinach
1 oz margarine
salt and pepper
pinch mixed herbs
pinch allspice
8 tablespoons breadcrumbs
2 beaten eggs

Wash the spinach thoroughly, then put into a large saucepan with a little salt, and cook slowly until it is tender. Then rub it through a sieve.

Melt the margarine in a saucepan, stir in the sieved spinach and season. Add the herbs, breadcrumbs, and beaten eggs, then blend well and put into a greased basin.

Cover with greased paper, and steam for 30–40 minutes until the mixture is firm. Serve with a white sauce.

Well, to his credit, Everard did make the effort, and the next day, when I called around to pick up my sink plunger, I could see the change in him right away. He'd cleaned the windows twice, and he'd even managed to tie his own shoelaces without going dizzy. And as for Slack, she was like a woman reborn.

'Slack,' I said, 'I haven't seen you looking like this since you won that donkey derby at Clacton, and you sang all the way home in the chara.'

'You're right,' she said, 'I feel like a woman reborn. Do you know when I first came out of hospital I just couldn't get interested in my stirrup pump again, but since Everard gave me some of your get up and go mould I've found that I can do wonders with it. In fact, I can squirt it further now than all the others, and what's more, I can fill a bucket in forty-five seconds.'

'Slack,' I said, 'I'm thrilled for you. Who would have thought when the war first started that you would have been pointing your nozzle on the roof of the Gem and defying Hitler to drop one. Keep up the good work, and spread the message to squirters everywhere. Tell them that if they want to strengthen their wrists, then try squirting on their rhubarb from a distance. And while they're at it, have a squirt over the neighbour's fence, it'll do wonders for the hollyhocks. Plus, why not have a stirrup pump competition to see who can squirt the highest up the wall?'

Well, I don't know whether she did or didn't because the next day I packed and left for my tour with *All Fun and Fluff*. And what a wonderful tour that was. We played all over the country, and it was a pleasure to see all those war-weary faces light up, and I used to think, 'what a pity Maud isn't here tonight, she's probably got the most war-weary face of the lot. I must go and cheer her up when I get back.'

HISTORIC PIE DISH FOR GUNS

THE villagers of Denby Dale, near Huddersfield, in response to the call for scrap metal are giving their historic iron pie-dish, which is 15ft. long and 5ft. wide.

One of the biggest Denby Dale pies was made in 1928 for a carnival in aid of Huddersfield Royal Infirmary. Five bullocks were baked in it, and it provided a plateful for 20,000. It cost £200 and weighed 35cwt.

— MADGE CUNCLIFFE —

For some reason I remember in particular the very last week we did with the show. It was at the Hippodrome, Acclesthorpe, and I stayed with Madge Cuncliffe – 25 shillings a week, bring your own sponge – and it was as if I'd never been away, nothing had changed, not even the tablecloth.

'Madge,' I said, 'how lovely to be back again. I haven't seen you since I was at the Hippodrome with *Peep Through My Porthole* twice nightly, matinees if wet. What a joy to see you. Tell me, are you still making the same gravy?'

'Yes,' she said. 'You can have it thick or thin.'

'Madge,' I said. 'You know me, I never complain either way, especially now there's a war on. Tell me, how is the parrot?'

'Lawrence,' she said, 'he passed away this very morning.'

'Never!' I said, 'he always seemed so perky. Although I do remember seeing him one morning lying flat on his back with his legs sticking up in the air, but I thought that was a trick. I'm sorry now that I didn't mention it at the time, maybe he was trying to tell us something.'

'Yes,' she said, 'that's how I found him this morning, but I've hidden the cage because I have all new people staying here this week, and I'd appreciate it if you didn't mention anything.'

'Madge,' I said, 'I know exactly how you must feel, and the last thing you want is to be reminded of it . . . there there, brave little woman.'

'Yes,' she said, looking at me strangely, 'and just a word to the wise. At dinner tonight, have the pie and *not* the chicken casserole. You'll enjoy the pie, I'm doing something special that my mother used to make during the First World War.'

'Madge,' I said, 'I shall look forward to that, and by the way how is your mother? Does she still go away on holidays to that nudist camp in Lytham St Anne's?'

'Yes,' she said. 'Isn't it amazing? She's eighty-three and never had nettle rash in her life. But she's thinking of giving it up, because her gentleman friend had a nasty touch of frostbite last year, and at the age of eighty-seven he says he doesn't want to push his luck.'

'Madge,' I said, 'at eighty-seven he's lucky to be pushing anything! But it just goes to show the wonderful spirit we have in this country, and that people even as old as your mother can still prance through the buttercups and daisies clinging to the good things in life, bully for her.'

Here is the dish that Madge served on that Monday night, and Tuesday, and Wednesday!

Trumper's Pie

½ cup brown breadcrumbs
4 oz cooked rice
1 large peeled and chopped tomato
1 chopped onion
2 cooked and sliced potatoes
1 oz ground nuts
1 tablespoon soaked tapioca
2 oz margarine
½ teaspoon mixed herbs of your choice
1 egg
salt and pepper, if desired

Line a greased pie dish with half the breadcrumbs. Mix the other ingredients, but keep half of the margarine.

Then put mixture into the dish, cover with the remainder of the breadcrumbs and margarine, and bake for almost 1 hour in a moderate oven.

Oh, I nearly forgot. Stick 8 oz pastry on top, and while it's baking, share a sherry with a friend.

GOODBYE MAUD

Yes, I had a wonderful week there, in spite of three days of trumper's pie followed by three days of black pudding and chips. But when I got back home I heard the sad news that the Vicar had gone down with mumps, and that Maud was about to pack up everything and go and live with her sister. I for one was very sorry to hear that Maud was leaving us. I thought of all the years she'd put in at the Gem, and all the years she'd spent with the girl guides before she had her knees seen to.

Yes, what memories of those far-off days she would be taking with her. Like the time she took them all out on a paper chase and they were lost for three days. And the time she took them on a day trip to Lake Windermere, but got on the wrong train and finished up at Loch Ness. I remember her saying afterwards, 'If only we had seen the monster it wouldn't have been so bad.' But that was Maud, she could even get lost walking to the Co-op.

Well, the first thing I did when I heard the news was to pop around and take her some little gifts.

'Maud,' I said, 'here are some jelly babies for the trip, and a little booklet called *How to Read a Street Map.* You might find it useful, because if you happen to lose your sister while you're out shopping, you don't want to spend the rest of the day wandering around the streets looking for her house.'

'Lawrence,' she said, 'I shall be too busy to get lost, because I'm starting work in a factory helping the war effort, I shall be parachuting.'

'Maud,' I said, 'surely they're not thinking of letting you jump at your age, to say nothing of your feet!'

'No,' she said, 'I'll be helping to make them. I used to be a dab hand with a needle and cotton, and they need people like me to sew up the fiddly bits.'

'Well,' I said, 'they've certainly chosen wisely, you've always been thorough in everything you've done. I remember how you were always repairing the seats at the Gem, and your sewing has always been a work of art. Good luck to you, I knew you'd come up trumps.'

Well, that night we all went around to Maud's for a little farewell drink, but it was a sad occasion really, because she had decided to travel light and insisted on giving back all the presents that we had given her on her retirement from the Gem. Slack got her ironing board and coal scuttle back. Lil got her set of cast-iron saucepans, and Everard and I took back the genuine plaster model of the Alsatian dog – not without difficulty, I might add.

As far as Bert's hawthorn cutting was concerned, Maud said she was going to leave it in the garden, because now that he had passed on to 'that great projection room in the sky' she was sure he'd be pleased if he ever looked down and saw how well it was doing. Mind you, she didn't say anything about the roll of nearly new lino he gave her, I think the woman next door had that.

Well, we couldn't let Maud go away without a little something, despite the fact that she wanted to travel light, so we all decided to give her one of our favourite recipes. Slack gave her one for curried eggs, Lil gave her one for mock suet balls, Everard gave her his recipe for gingerbread biscuits, and I gave her one I had made up especially, called change of luck pudding.

I remember Slack turning to me afterwards and saying, 'Wouldn't it be smashing if your pudding really did change her luck, and wouldn't it be lovely if she suddenly met a nice gentleman friend at the factory, someone in the same position as herself, you know, a bit crippled. It could happen, you know.'

'Slack,' I said, 'you're all heart. Always thinking of other people's happiness. I remember the time when that little boy down the road lost his frog, and you sat out in your garden all night trying to catch him another one, and I had to help carry you in the next morning. Come along Slack, let's say our farewells to Maud, and sleep happy with the thought that she'll always remember us whenever she makes up one of our recipes.'

Yes, and these are the very recipes that Maud took with her to start her new life.

Slack's Curried Eggs
(for four people)

1½ oz margarine
1 chopped onion
1 oz flour
1 teaspoon curry powder
½ pint stock
1 small chopped apple
1 teaspoon desiccated coconut
some sultanas
4 hot hard-boiled eggs

Melt the margarine, add the chopped onion and fry until brown. Stir in the flour and curry powder and continue to cook for a few minutes. Add the stock, chopped apple, coconut, and sultanas, and simmer gently until the onion is cooked.

Cut the eggs in half, and arrange them on a bed of well-cooked rice, then pour the curry sauce over them.

Lil's Mock Suet Balls

4 oz flour
4 oz oatmeal
4 oz grated raw potatoes
¼ teacup water
½ teaspoon salt
½ teaspoon baking powder

Mix fairly dry, then roll into balls. Drop them into your boiling soup or stew, and cook for 45 minutes.

Everard's Gingerbread Biscuits

2 oz margarine
8 oz flour
2 oz brown sugar
½ oz ground ginger
4 oz treacle

Rub the margarine into the flour, add the sugar and ginger. Then warm the treacle and mix that with the other ingredients. Roll out thin and cut into shapes, and bake in a moderate oven for about 15 minutes.

Change of Luck Pudding

4 oz chopped apples
2 oz currants
3 oz sugar
4 oz breadcrumbs
2 oz suet
1 well-beaten egg
½ teacup milk
1 lemon

Mix the ingredients well together, and boil for 2 hours in a greased basin covered with greased paper.

And, as well as the recipes, Slack had written a special going away poem. It was one of those poems that seemed to say it all.

Goodbye Dear Maud

Goodbye dear Maud, you're going
And we wish you all good cheer.
Tho' not all of you is going,
You have left some memories here.

Goodbye old friend, keep smiling,
And let's hope we'll meet again.
And just for once, this Monday,
Try and get on the right train!

Goodbye dear Maud, best wishes,
You'll be always in our thoughts.
Don't forget your tin of 'Fiery Jack'
And your jar of smelling salts.

Goodbye old friend, we'll miss you,
As they'll miss you at the Gem,
For the time you spent repairing seats,
Time and time again.

Yes, the patron's won't forget you,
You'll be always on their mind,
Especially when they sit there,
With a spring up their behind!

Love from Slack, Lil, Everard, Lawrence, and all the gang.

Maud took it all in good part, and that was the last we saw of her. It was Faith Gudgeon who took her to the station the next morning, and that was a mistake for a start! What happened was Faith went first and took Maud's luggage on to the train, the train suddenly started, Maud was left on the platform, and Faith finished up ten stops down the line. But they sorted it out eventually, and we had a postcard from Maud saying that she had arrived safely, although she had had a slight delay, because while she was on the train there was an air raid, and they were shunted into a siding for the night. She said she was comfortable, because two sailors wrapped her in a blanket and lifted her up on to the luggage rack, but she didn't get all that much sleep because they were playing cards all night, and she couldn't take much of an interest, because the cigarette smoke was a bit thick up where she was. But she said that they did open the window now and again, and she could hear the rippling of a nearby stream, so that was a bit comforting. Anyway, she said she now felt as fit as a fiddle and hoped we all were too.

TRY AN EEL DIET

So Nourishing

THE Ministry of Agriculture and Fisheries are being urged to establish a big fish-farming industry.

People who have seen big fish farms in Denmark, Holland, and Germany, suggest farming trout.

No, say the Ministry, go and catch eels. Trout would cost 2s. 3d. each to farm and take three years to grow.

Few parts of Britain, indeed, are suitable to the farming of any fish.

But eels, said a Ministry official yesterday, are infinitely more nutritious than trout.

"And millions of them are just waiting to be caught and eaten in East Anglia, the Fens, Sussex, Kent, and many other parts of the country.

"In the autumn they will be making their way to the sea. They should not be allowed to get away. They are first-class food."

The Ministry, he added, means to organise demonstrations of the best ways of catching eels.

A QUICK YODEL

Yes it was a sad day when Maud left us, but life went on. I remember lying in the bath squirting the water out of my rubber duck, and thinking 'I'm sure that hole is getting bigger' when suddenly I felt the urge to yodel again.

You see, at one time I was very keen on yodelling, and in fact I even went out and bought myself a Tyrolean hat with a feather stuck in it. And every spare moment I would climb the nearest hillock and give a 'Yo-del-a-ee-dee'. But then one day while I was out yodelling with a friend, my voice suddenly took a turn for the worse. My 'yo' was alright, but I had a lot of trouble with my 'del', and as far as my 'a-ee-dee' was concerned, that disappeared right up the canyon!

Well, I stopped squeezing the soap into funny shapes, and thought, 'I know, I'll make one of my favourite recipes, Swiss eggs. If that doesn't do anything for my yodel nothing will.'

Well, it was amazing. After just one mouthful I could feel my yodel coming back, and I've never lost it since, so why not try some, and if you feel in the mood why not have a little yodel tonight before you go to sleep?

Swiss Eggs (for four people)

1½ oz margarine
3 oz Gruyère cheese
4 eggs
a little nutmeg
a little allspice
salt and pepper
3 tablespoons evaporated milk

Melt half the margarine in a pie dish, then put in a thin layer of cheese, and break the eggs on top.

Add the seasoning, and pour on the evaporated milk, followed by the remainder of the grated cheese.

Place some pats of margarine on top, and bake in a slow oven for 15–20 minutes.

Yo-del-a-ee-dee!

— SLACK'S RHUBARB —

A few days later while I was still relaxing my larynx, I suddenly heard a rat-ta-tat-tat on my knocker. 'Friend or foe?' I cried, as I leapt into my 'Red Shadow' dressing-gown. Well, it was Faith Gudgeon.

'Faith,' I said, 'what on earth is the matter? You look like something the cat's brought in. You're obviously in a state of flux, so sit yourself down and have some blancmange.'

'No,' she said. 'My hands are too shaky for that. You see, I've just found something nasty behind the piano.'

'Faith,' I said, 'what's the world coming to? It must have been there since your last party. Maybe it's an old doughnut, or one of your sponge fingers.'

'No,' she said, 'whatever it is, it's coming up between the floorboards. Do you think it could be something from outer space?'

'Well, if it was from outer space,' I said, 'surely it would come in through the roof. But hang on a minute, I'll find my chopper and we'll sort it out.'

Well of course, you've guessed, it was Slack's rhubarb on the move again.

'Oh!' said Faith when I told her. 'It must have been attracted by my piano playing.' I thought, 'If you believe that you'll believe anything.'

'Don't worry about it,' I said. 'I'll give it the chop, then I'll go around and tell Slack about it. Now then, you hold it up while I chop it off, and if you don't want to look, then close your eyes.'

Well, it only took a couple of minutes, then I made Faith a cup of beef tea and left her lying limp in the back parlour.

Then I made my way to Slack's house, and there she was, polishing the front step as usual – I don't know why, because she was forever slipping on it.

'Slack,' I said, 'did you know your rhubarb is spreading again? You must do something about it, it's coming up in all sorts of strange places.'

'Don't worry,' she said, 'I've just seen a poster urging us all to dig for victory, and the first thing I'm going to do is dig up my rhubarb, then I'm going to plant all sorts of vegetables instead.'

'Slack,' I said, 'it'll be another first for you. Do you remember you were the first one down this street to put up your blackout curtains, and that surprised everyone, especially the baker; he didn't call for a fortnight, he thought you were dead! Yes, Slack,' I said, 'go to it, but don't go as mad as you usually do. The last time you dug up your garden, you went so deep you struck water.'

Mind you, that was in a fit of temper because the council had sent her a letter to say that her garden was so overgrown they were afraid that one day she'd go out there to hang up her washing, get lost in the undergrowth, and they would have to send out a native tracker to find her. But they weren't serious, it was just someone at the town hall having a little joke. Besides, where would they find a native tracker around here?

'Get out there, Slack,' I told her, 'and do your bit. With your green fingers you'll probably finish up with the world's biggest vegetables.'

'Yes,' she said. 'But I want everyone to join in, I want to see every garden chock-a-block with veg, so I've written a poem which I'm going to push through every door, and if they don't start digging then I shall want to know the reason why.'

She certainly had the bit between her teeth that day, and this is the poem that she pushed through every letterbox she could find. And, of course, it was called 'Dig for Victory'.

LOAVES—FOUR SHAPES ONLY NOW

HOUSEWIVES from August 26 will have only four types of loaf to choose from.

There are at present 45 different shapes in England. The standard shapes will be tin loaves, ovenbottom loaves, sandwich loaves, and what is known in Scotland as a batch loaf.

Loaves must weigh 1lb. or an even number of pounds, except in Scotland, where a tin loaf of 1lb. 12oz. will be allowed.

Bakers will also be permitted to sell a Vienna loaf of 8oz. and rolls not exceeding 2oz. Fruit bread can be sold without restriction as to weight.

The restrictions will economise labour and baking capacity, and reduce waste. They are recommended by the trade.

The manufacturer of special types of bread of a low starch content can apply to the Food Ministry for a special licence to continue to make them without restriction or weight.

Dig for Victory

We have to dig for victory,
We have to grow our own,
We need those leeks and cabbages,
The seeds must all be sown.

We need potatoes from the soil,
We need peas from their pods,
So dig up all your garden lawns,
Get rid of all those sods.

Get out there in your wellies,
Be the weather fair or foul,
Forget for once your aches and pains,
Get planting with your trowel.

Now let's all dig for victory,
Let's show the others how,
So get up off your backsides,
Not tomorrow, do it now!

Well, of course, the next day Slack went straight out into the garden, trod on a rake, and had a black eye for three weeks. But at least she made the effort.

Our Slack was a wonder. In fact, I don't know how she managed to pull it all in, because she was back working at the Gem, plus doing her bit of firewatching, and yet her vegetables shot up more or less overnight, and she was out there every spare moment.

I remember saying to her, 'Slack, I don't know how you find the energy. I hope you don't overtax yourself and have a relapse, we don't want you poorly again.'

'Laz,' she said, 'every time I go out into the garden and see my marrows it makes it all worth while. You see, I want to give the Vicar a surprise at the Harvest Festival this year, because last year it was hardly worth his while opening the church. He only took in three bundles of rhubarb, two cucumbers and a tin of baked beans, and it's no wonder he whisked through the service. I felt so embarrassed. No sooner had I sat down than it was time to get up again.'

'Now look,' I said, 'over the years you've given more to the church than anyone. Look at the time they were collecting jam-jars, your name was always top of the list. And when the old Vicar was alive you were always taking his boots to the mender's. And I know for a fact that the last five years he was alive you were the one who darned his socks and cut his hair. You see, Slack, it's the little things that matter in life. You don't have to give the Vicar a big marrow, I'm sure he'd be happy with a gherkin as long as it was given in the right spirit.'

But of course Slack was determined and beavered away until, sure enough, come the Harvest Festival, there she was outside the church with the biggest marrow I've ever seen, and I've seen a few in my life I can tell you.

'Slack,' I said, 'you've certainly got a winner there, I bet you can't wait to have it blessed, and to think you grew it from a seed.'

And credit where credit's due, how many other people would have climbed out of their air-raid shelters twice a night to water it?

But of course it was such a beauty that the Vicar couldn't bring himself to take it away from her. 'Share it with a friend,' he said, after he had blessed it. And it was those very words that inspired Slack to write this poem.

Share a Marrow with a Friend

If you ever grow a marrow,
Which is far too big for you,
Then find a friend to share it,
There'll be plenty there for two.

Above all, don't be greedy,
And don't act before you think,
If you only eat one half of it,
The other half will shrink.

So now that there's a war on,
Prepare your sharpest knife,
And give your friend the biggest bit,
You'll be her friend for life.

Slack entered this poem in a Dig for Victory competition and won a hundredweight sack of compost, but when she tried to lift it, her left leg went.

'Bubbles' Broadbent who appeared with me in 'Tickle your Aunt with a Feather'. I think someone was frying onions in the next dressing-room.

Apricot Lil closing the doors of the look-out post on top of the Gem cinema before going into the projection room to help Percy unwind.

'Badger' Hawkins, who taught Everard how to knit.

— NELSON THE RABBIT —

I remember going round to see Slack about a week later. She was all red-eyed and a mere shadow of her former self.

'Slack,' I said, 'what's happening? Don't tell me your leg's still throbbing, Dr Tizzard said you were coming on well.'

'No', she said, 'my leg's alright, but something happened this morning and it's put me right back. Someone very close passed away during the night.'

'Slack,' I said, 'surely not Mr Belvedere, I saw him chopping wood only the day before yesterday. He looked a bit flushed but I didn't think he'd go as quickly as that!'

'No,' she said, 'not Mr Belvedere – Nelson, my rabbit. I found him huddled in his hutch this morning when I went to give him his breakfast, and I'd had him ever since he was a bundle of fluff. I should have looked after him better.'

'Slack,' I said, trying hard to stop her sobbing, 'nobody could have done more for Nelson than you did. You were his whole life, you even made a black velvet patch to put over his blind eye.'

'I know,' she said, 'but I can't bring myself to bury him in the garden, it just doesn't seem right to put him in the earth.'

'Slack,' I said, 'you can't very well bury him at sea even if today *is* Trafalgar Day. Look, I read somewhere that when the Egyptian kings were buried they used to bury food with them to see them on their journey to the other side, and Nelson really loved that piece of marrow you gave him, so what finer gesture than to bury him with one of your marrows. The rabbits on the other side will think he's a king, and he'll be pleased as well, and I'm sure that when you meet him again in the other world he'll turn and say, "Thank you for the marrow".'

'Laz,' she said, drying her eyes, 'you're right. I never looked at it like that before, you've put my mind at rest.'

'Slack,' I said, 'it's all a matter of believing. Now then, chin up, he's going to a land where the carrots are six feet tall and the lettuce leaves are the size of football pitches. Come along,' I said, 'we'll lay him to rest, have two minutes' silence, then pop down to the Cock and Trumpet and the drinks are on me.'

Well, I've never seen so much drink go down one throat; it was like standing next to the Niagara Falls.

'Slack,' I said, 'ease up, I know you're trying to forget, but the way you're going you'll finish up forgetting your own name!'

Still, who could blame her, and at least she slept well that night, and I'm pleased to say that the next day she was almost back to the Slack we all knew and loved.

After that, I didn't see her for quite a while though, until one day I was walking through the woods looking for some pine cones to paint silver for my Christmas tree, and all of a sudden who should I see but Slack walking towards me, carrying a sack of chestnuts.

'Slack,' I said, 'don't tell me you're going into business this Christmas!'

'No,' she said, 'but the other day I was taking up some old lino in my spare room, and underneath was an old newspaper with a recipe inside for chestnut soup, so I thought I'd have a go.'

'You've got enough chestnuts there to start a soup kitchen,' I told her, 'I'm sure you won't need all of those.'

Well, of course, when she read the recipe again she realised that she didn't need a sackful, so she gave some to Mr Belvedere to roast while he was on Home Guard duty, and some to the man from the council who had called around to look at her overflow. And seeing all those chestnuts suddenly reminded me of one of my favourite prewar songs, 'Underneath the Spreading Chestnut Tree', and I remembered all the hours I had spent trying to teach Everard the actions, and trying to teach Slack, who was even worse! I was surprised at Slack, because working at the Gem she must have seen the King and Queen doing it dozens of times on the newsreels.

But at least Slack got it right when it came to making the chestnut soup, and here is that recipe which had been under her lino all those years.

Chestnut Soup

$1\frac{1}{2}$ lb chestnuts
1 small onion
4 stalks celery
1 quart stock
teaspoon lemon juice
a little allspice
salt and pepper
1 oz flour
1 oz margarine
$\frac{1}{2}$ pint evaporated milk (optional)

Cut the end off each chestnut, then bake in a hot oven for a few moments or boil for about 20 minutes, then remove the outer and inner skins.

Put the chestnuts, sliced onion and celery into a saucepan, and add the stock, lemon juice and seasoning.

Simmer for about $1\frac{1}{2}$ hours or until the chestnuts are tender, then pass through a sieve.

Blend the flour with a little water, and add to the soup along with the margarine.

Stir and bring to the boil, and just before serving add the evaporated milk, if desired.

But as well as the chestnut soup, what really surprised me was Everard's wartime Christmas cake. You see he had been on about it since the summer, because he wanted to get it made so he could put it away in an airtight tin, and I remember the first time he mentioned it.

'Lawrence,' he said, 'I want to get cracking, because the longer it stands the better it is.'

'Everard,' I said, 'you've just broken my dream . . . but carry on, what were you saying?'

'Well,' he said, 'I'm going to scrounge around for a little bit here and a little bit there until I manage to get all of the ingredients. Then I shall make an early start.'

Well, of course, I went around to see him a couple of weeks later and his kitchen looked like a battlefield. 'Everard,' I said, 'you must get some method in your kitchen, there are more raisins on the floor than there are on the table, and I can't imagine what your prunes are doing lying in that black treacle! Even your self-raising has gone lumpy. You'll have to pull your socks up. Surely you were never like this in the cookery classes at Clattern Road Council School. You told me you came away with honours, but I'm beginning to have my doubts. I know you're very good when it comes to making little fruity cakes, but your mind seems to go limp if you get a recipe with more than six ingredients. You're a typical Aries, you start off with all the enthusiasm in the world, and then you suddenly fall off, and I won't always be behind you to give you that final push, you know. So come along, put down that cooking sherry and hand me the recipe, or Christmas will be come and gone before you even get it in the oven.'

Mind you, to be truthful, I only read out the instructions, and he made the actual cake, and all credit to him for producing one of the finest cakes that I ever tasted during the war.

To the Country People of Britain

YOU have a great duty — the duty of keeping the roads free for our troops, no matter what happens.

Should parachutists land, or should enemy forces push inland from our coasts, some less-brave people may be tempted to flee from threatened villages and towns.

Don't do it. Stay where you are. This is not just advice, it is an order from the Government. The greatest harm any man or woman could do to Britain at such a time would be to clutter up the roads, and so hinder our own troops advancing to drive the enemy out.

In France refugees crowding the roads made it impossible for the army to bring up reinforcements. So France was lost !

This must not happen here. Remember, you will be far safer from bombing and machine-gunning downstairs in your own home than you would be on the open roads.

Remember, too, the Home Guard will be defending your village, and the Army will be defending your country. They need the roads.

...that's why you must **STAY PUT**

Everard's Wartime Christmas Cake

8 oz margarine
3 oz lard
2 oz brown sugar pieces
2 oz black treacle
2 oz golden syrup
$\frac{1}{2}$ teaspoon mixed spice
$\frac{1}{2}$ teaspoon grated nutmeg
$\frac{1}{2}$ teaspoon salt
small tin sweetened milk
4 eggs
1 tablespoon rum or sherry
juice of 1 lemon
1 lb self-raising flour
water to mix
1 lb sultanas or raisins
8 oz currants
4 oz peel
4 oz chopped dates
4 oz soaked chopped prunes

Beat together the margarine, lard, sugar, treacle and syrup. Then add the spices, salt, and tinned milk and mix well.

Beat the eggs with the rum or sherry and lemon juice, and add to the mixture along with the flour and enough water to make it moist. Wash all the fruit, and add it to the mixture.

Line one large greased cake tin with two thicknesses of greased paper, and put in the cake mixture.

Tie brown paper around the outside of the tin, and set the tin on a baking sheet covered with a thick layer of sand.

Start the cake in a moderate oven, and reduce the heat every 15 minutes during the first hour (do not open oven door). Continue baking for a further 2 hours on a low temperature, and to judge whether the cake is cooked, hold the tin near your ear, and when it stops making a slight singing noice, it is ready.

Allow it to partly cool in the tin, then turn out carefully on to a cooling tray, then store in a tin – well wrapped in some greaseproof paper – until required.

BE NICE TO YOUR COALMAN

The first week of January 1942 was one of the bleakest I remember.

I was lying on my rug in front of the fire, thinking 'I wonder how long my Welsh nuts will last out? I've seen neither sight nor sound of the coalman, I wonder if he's topped up Everard yet?'

Well, I should have guessed. Everard was in a worse state than I was, and the only thing that was keeping him going was some coal-dust brickettes and an old railway sleeper.

'Everard, you haven't been upsetting the coalman again, have you?' I asked. 'I've been waiting all week for him to drop his nuts, and my coal cupboard is bare. Only I know what you're like. You can't stand anyone with grubby hands, but you know as well as I do that it's no good standing at the door holding out your nail file and a jar of cold cream. He's selling coal not lace handkerchiefs. I know what started it, mind you; you were alright with him until that day last summer when he made that comment about your new curtains, but you have to live with a bit of criticism these days. People like him aren't going to touch their forelocks for you. He's got something you want, not the other way around. So let's start a Be Nice to Your Coalman Week and we'll all benefit. Next time you see him in the street, beckon him over, offer him one of your savouries and pat his horse a few times. And do try not to lose your temper if he only lets you have one sack, because standing there with your arms folded and stamping your foot only makes him worse. And next Christmas try to think of some little gift that's a bit different; the whole world gives him soap!'

Well, for once Everard took my advice and baked some little savouries, and it's amazing but overnight the coalman changed into a different person. It just goes to show how a little thought can fill your coal cupboard, helped, of course, by some little leek and tomato savouries.

Leek and Tomato Savoury
(for your coalman)

1 bundle leeks	½ pint white sauce
8 oz skinned tomatoes	some breadcrumbs
3 oz grated cheese	seasoning

Wash the leeks and prepare in the usual way.

Place half of them lengthwise in a greased deep dish, then cover with halves of tomatoes and sprinkle with some grated cheese, and repeat the process.

Pour the white sauce over and sprinkle the top with grated cheese and breadcrumbs.

Bake in a moderate oven for 20–30 minutes.

Of course, the one person who never went short of coal during the war was Vera Titsall. Her boiler was always on the go. You see, Vera's ex-husband was an engine driver, and they were daggers drawn, and every day she would go down to the level crossing, and as his train passed, she would shout at him and give him the 'V' sign. Then he'd give her the 'V' sign back, pick up the biggest piece of coal he could put his hands on and chuck it at her. Mind you, she had concussion twice, but her boiler never went out, and not many people could say that.

I think one of the reasons that Vera and her husband never got on was his liking for prunes, because Vera couldn't stand them. She said to me once, 'Every time I touch a prune I feel as if I'm handling something that's been mummified.'

I said, 'Vera, think yourself lucky, Ada Tichburn's husband is like that all over! As Ada says, "Stick a prune down his trousers and you'd have a job to find it." But that's Ada for you; never one to mince words!'

Anyway, I've always loved prunes, and what better dish for the prune lover than a prune snowball with rose sauce?

Prune Snowball with Rose Sauce

4 oz boiled unpolished rice
1 teacup prunes, soaked overnight

Line a greased basin with half the rice, then pour in the prunes. Place a layer of rice on top, then cover with greased paper and steam for 1 hour. Turn out and serve.

Rose Sauce

1 small boiled beetroot
½ pint water
1 small lemon
8 oz sugar
¼ teaspoon vanilla

Peel the beetroot and cut into small slices. Boil in cold water with rind of lemon for 30 minutes.

Strain, and return juice to pan along with the sugar, vanilla, and the juice of the lemon. Boil for 5 minutes and serve hot.

Now, another great prune lover was my good friend Crispin Touche, ex-chef at the Queen's Hotel. You couldn't forget his prune snowballs and what a joy they were.

The first time I ever tried them was just before the war on a wet Guy Fawkes' night. I remember we were both sitting eating them in a deserted bandstand and trying in vain to light his damp sparkler – which reminds me, he still owes me for a roman candle and a catherine wheel – but despite all that I remember him best for his steamed scrap bread pudding. You see, when Crispin was chef at the Queen's, he made his mark by going for the unusual. In fact, the guests never quite knew what to expect from him, and many is the time that the whole dining-room has stood up and requested – nay demanded – to see the chef.

Still, Crispin was never one to seek praise from the patrons, he preferred to stay in the background beavering away to satisfy their jaded palates, but of course always keeping economy in mind. As Crispin once said to me, 'Anyone can prepare a banquet, but how many can serve up superb steamed scrap bread pudding?' How true.

Crispin Touche's Steamed Bread Pudding

8 oz crusts or small stale pieces bread
3 heaped tablespoons chopped suet
3 level tablespoons sugar
3 level tablespoons washed and picked currants
1 level tablespoon chopped peel
1 teaspoon ground ginger
½ teaspoon mixed spice
1 teaspoon bicarbonate of soda
a little milk
1 egg

Soak the bread in cold water until soft, then squeeze dry and crumble with a fork. Mix all the dry ingredients, except the soda, together.

Mix the soda with a little milk, then add it with the egg to the dry ingredients. Mix well together, and put into a greased basin. Cover with greased paper and steam for at least 2 hours.

Turn out, and serve with a custard of your choice.

Yes, what a delightful pudding, and what a pity that Crispin was now miles away making new friends with his magic touch, especially now that meat was getting a bit short.

A few days later I saw Slack at the shops, and she was picking here and picking there. 'Hello, Slack,' I said, 'how are you getting on for meat these days?'

'Laz,' she said, 'don't ask me. I've just been in to see Freddie Fillet, and all he's got is some pig's feet and a bit of breast. But it's not his fault, he can't give you what he hasn't got. Big Ethel was in there too and she was having a right old moan. "Oh," she was saying, "I remember a time when he would practically go down on his hands and knees to try and get you to have some of his 'best end', and he always gave you a cracker at Christmas if you showed any interest in his rump. It's amazing how things have changed in here now there's a war on." '

Well, Slack was really annoyed with Big Ethel. As soon as she got home she sat down and wrote one of her poems, which she sent off to the local paper. It was called 'Be Kind to your Butcher', and here it is.

Freddie Fillet's butcher's shop where Apricot Lil used to go every Sunday morning to roll his faggots and twist his chipolatas.

Be Kind to Your Butcher

Always be kind to your butcher,
He can only do his best,
If he hasn't got a thick end,
Then have a bit of breast.

Please be kind to your butcher,
If he says that's all he's got,
Don't look at it disdainfully,
And complain 'That's not a lot.'

And even if he promised
That he had a little treat,
Don't peep behind the counter
For that special bit of meat.

Remember there are other folks,
Behind you in the queue,
There'd be murder if he whipped it out,
And said, 'This is for you.'

So always be kind to your butcher,
And when this war is won,
He'll give you all the meat you want,
You'll think your birthday's come.

Slack was thinking of writing one called 'Be Kind to Your Grocer' but she found out that he'd slipped Vera Titsall a tin of pineapple chunks, so she didn't bother. That's Slack!

But of course Apricot Lil didn't think much of the poem, because she'd fallen out with Freddie Fillet all that time ago. And the only man in her life now was Percy, especially as he was now living in her spare room. I remember calling around to see them one Sunday morning, and there they were sitting at the kitchen table making sheep's eyes at each other over a cup of Bovril.

'Lawrence,' she said, 'I want you to be the first to know, Percy and myself are to become as one. We're getting engaged next week, war or no war.'

'Lil,' I said, 'I'm agog, what a nice surprise. It's what you've always wanted for yourself, the steady hand on your shoulder, the comforting word in your ear, and someone who will scratch your back when you can't reach the spot that itches. It'll do wonders for your nerves as well, think of all the money you'll save once you get off all those tablets, and no more cold baths and night starvation. It'll be the making of both of you, and when one of you catches a cold, at least you'll have someone to share it with. Yes, you're doing the right thing, and Percy's certainly looking better since you've been looking after him. I've never seen him looking so full in the face.'

'Yes,' she said. 'But I must try to make him a few more exotic dishes, because now we're getting engaged I think we might try a few more spicy things instead of the usual. Mind you, Percy says he's very fond of my fritters, and he doesn't think that he'll ever get fed up with them, but I think it would be nice if I offered him a bit of variety, don't you?'

'Lil,' I said, 'you do what you want. It's your choice, and you know best how to hold your man. Every man is that little bit different. By all means give him something he's never had, but don't kill him with kindness. When he says he's had enough, back off, the last thing you want to give him is indigestion.'

— MAUD'S GENTLEMAN — FRIEND

Mind you, that wasn't the only romance that was in the air that year, because Slack called around to see me a couple of days later and she was quite chirpy.

'Laz,' she said, 'I've just had a letter from Maud, and she's met a gentleman at last. She says he's very mature, and he plays the banjo in his spare time, so she's taken up the piano again. She says that they've been practising, and already they have six tunes which they can play together. She says they have been asked to play in the factory canteen one lunchtime to entertain the workers, but she's a bit worried because she's never played in front of the public before, and it's a bit different from playing in your own front room when you know that the next-door neighbour is deaf. But she says that her gentleman friend is giving her a lot of confidence because he plays the banjo very loud, so even if she did play a couple of wrong notes she doubts if anyone would hear them. In fact, she says he plays so loud that she can't even hear what she's playing, and she's nearer to the piano than anybody!

'Maud says that when she gets to know him a bit better she's going to ask him to take the edge off it a bit, and give her a fighting chance, but at the moment she's not saying much because she doesn't want him to think that she's got stars in front of her eyes and is crying out to be another Charlie Kunz. Still, she says that she thinks he'll be alright when she tells him, because they've had a couple of fish suppers together and she's getting to know him quite well. He has mentioned something about a war wound from the First World War, but it doesn't show, and she's wondering where it is. He seems to walk alright, which is just as well, because she thinks she may have to go into hospital again to have her knee seen to, and he'll be someone to lean on.'

'Bully for her,' I said. 'Maud's gone through a lot in her lifetime and she deserves some sunshine at the end. Do you remember when she was besotted with that window cleaner from Jasmine Street, and how she found out that he was forever popping in to see Cissie Turnbull, and how he made out that she only invited him in so that he could give her his opinion of her buttered fudge? And then there was that other man who was a turncock for the water company, and didn't he let her down badly? And nobody could have done more for him than Maud. She was always putting his socks through her wringer and drying his boots in front of her fire. I remember saying to her at the time, "Maud, you're a fool to yourself. I'm the last one to interfere, but I think you should be told. To put it bluntly, I know for a fact that you're not the only one he shows his chilblains to. No names, no pack drill, but a word to the wise, next time he comes squelching up to your front door, tell him your wringer has broken and your fire has gone out. See how interested he is then!"'

Yes, and it was true. I remember Maud turning round at the time and saying, 'Lawrence, you're right. I think I knew it all along, but I just didn't want to believe it. He was always coming around for a bite, but now he can whistle up another street.'

And do you know, she didn't seem to be that upset. She invited me to sit down and have my first taste of scalloped roes, and if you like your roes scalloped then this is the recipe for you.

Remember, the next time you go in to see your friendly fishmonger, don't dabble with his dabs, or linger near his lobster, just ask him for a pound of soft roes and four scallop shells, and you'll have one of the most nourishing dishes possible. Maud and I had two each that day and made real pigs of ourselves, but why not?

BLACK-OUT BREAKERS MAY ALL BE GAOLED

PEOPLE who don't black-out properly will in future run a bigger risk of being sent to prison.

Magistrates everywhere—and especially in London — are seriously concerned at the steady increase in the numbers of cases coming before them, and are determined to stop such offences.

Fining is proving an inadequate deterrent, there have been instances of people being fined over and over again.

The common excuse, "I didn't know a light was showing," is no longer likely to result in getting off with the payment of a few pounds. The punishment will now more often be imprisonment "without the option."

Magistrates have the power to impose a sentence up to three months or a fine not exceeding £100—or both. Offenders indicted may find themselves sent to prison for two years or fined £500—or both.

Maud's Scalloped Roes

a few breadcrumbs
1 lb soft roes
$\frac{1}{2}$ pint white sauce
salt and pepper
mashed potato

Grease the four scallop shells and line with the breadcrumbs.

Lightly poach the roes and cut into medium-sized pieces. Divide into four portions, and place one portion in each scallop shell. Cover with the white sauce, then sprinkle breadcrumbs on top, season, and make an edging of mashed potato around the edge of each shell.

Bake in a hot oven until golden brown on top.

If you can't get fresh roes, you can always use tinned, it's the same difference.

Anyway, a few days later I made two scalloped roes for Everard, and he was over the moon when he tasted them. You see, Everard has always liked something a little bit different – for instance, he was the first person down his street to try a Bounty bar – and I knew that he would come up with a dainty little dish for me to try, and I was right.

This is a recipe which was given to him years ago by his trampoline instructor whilst they were jumping up and down. Everard said he had a bit of difficulty writing it down while suspended in mid-air, but it was such a simple recipe he made it without looking at his notes.

Minced Chicken and Poached Eggs on Spinach

left-over cold chicken
left-over stuffing
a little flour
a little milk
2 tablespoons spinach per person
1 egg per person

Mince the remains of the cold chicken and stuffing, and then stew the bones and skin for about an hour in enough cold water to half cover them. Strain, return stock to the saucepan and thicken with a little blended flour and milk. Bring the mixture to the boil, and add the minced chicken and stuffing.

Mince the raw spinach, and cook it in one tablespoon of water. Poach the eggs.

Arrange a border of spinach on a dish, put the minced chicken in the centre and the poached eggs on top.

Try it, it could do wonders for your trampolining.

— THE GRAND TICKLE — YOUR FANCY COMPETITION

Well, shortly after that I went on tour with my Strolling Players. We were doing two wonderful plays, *Lust in the Dust* and *Nanook of the North*, and many people said that my Nanook was the best they'd seen since before the war. So of course when I got back home I thought I must go and tell Everard about my success, it may spur him on to perform again.

Well, when I called on him, his front room looked as if he was getting ready to move.

'Everard,' I said, 'what on earth are you doing? You've emptied every drawer and cupboard! Don't tell me you're being evacuated!'

'No,' he said, 'I'm trying to raise something for the Vicar. He's having a jumble sale for the restoration fund, and he's just discovered that he's got woodworm in his vestry.'

'Never!' I said. 'That's worse than having bats in your belfry. What can I do to help?'

'Well,' he said, 'sort out your old knicks and your old knacks and take them along to the Vicar. I've already found my old roller skates and my duck warbler, and now I'm looking for my tambourine. You know, the one I was presented with for my rendering of "Jesus wants me for a Sunbeam".'

'Everard,' I said, 'I'm sure I've something tucked away that would help the Vicar, there must be something that I shall never use again.'

And of course there was. There were the riding boots I wore in that marvellous dramatic play, *The Reluctant Huntsman* or *The Man who wouldn't Mount*, plus the snowshoes I wore in *Three Months up the Klondyke*, and the stuffed ferret that played an important role in a very moving play called *The Ferret that Never Knew its Mother*.

Well, the Vicar was more than pleased. In fact, after the jumble sale he invited me back to the vicarage for a cup of tea and a whirligig cake. When we were sitting down and the tea had been poured he turned to me and said, 'Lawrence, I am toying with the idea of holding a Grand Tickle Your Fancy Competition to try and entice more people to take an active part in the church activities. You see, a lot of people have been dropping off lately. Did you know, for instance, last week we only had three people turn up for our knitting circle, and last evening only one person turned up for my lecture on the effects of gastric juices on the camels of the Nile delta: April 1906.'

'Vicar,' I said, 'I *am* surprised. Obviously the word hadn't been put about. When they showed *The Son of the Sheik* at the Gem you couldn't get in for love nor money, even Slack Alice had to climb in through the window of the ladies' and she was working there! But never mind, tell me more about the competition.'

'Well,' he went on, 'I would like everyone to conjure up their favourite dish, then hopefully I will be able to get the Mayoress to judge them and award a prize for the tastiest. I was thinking of giving a cash prize at first, but on reflection it may be distasteful to some, and so I am donating a prize of a more uplifting nature – namely, a pew with a view, and a new hymnbook bound in genuine imitation red leather.'

'Vicar,' I said, 'they'll be racing to their cookers, what a good idea. I may go mad and do one of my upside-down cakes, and I'm sure Everard will make one of his feather puddings, plus I'll have a word with Slack Alice and see if she can write you one of her poems to stick on the noticeboard. Leave it to me.'

Well, of course, when I told Slack about it all, she sat straight down and wrote a poem. Then she dashed out to her kitchen to make her 'fancy'.

I realised afterwards that I'd forgotten to tell her what the prize was. Ah well! Here is her poem.

Tickle Your Fancy

If you're sick of the sight of a faggot,
And fed up with fishcakes and peas,
Then have something that tickles your fancy,
Something cheerful that's certain to please.

Try a cockle and cucumber sandwich,
Or scallops with lots of brown bread,
Or sprats that are done nice and cripsy,
I know someone who eats them in bed.

Why not a delicious sponge finger?
Or a cluster of tiny mince pies?
Or a suggestion, if today is your birthday,
Why not try a banana surprise?

I've had dreams of Rudolph Valentino,
And I've gone all exotic of late,
So I'm having a Bedouin supper,
Half a lamb's heart, three figs and a date.

So come on and tickle your fancy,
And let's see a smile on your face,
'Cos if we can still smile with a war on,
Then there's hope for the whole human race.

Well, on the great day itself, it was amazing how many turned up with their 'fancies', and here are just a few of them.

Vera Titsall – *Fricassee of Haricot Beans*

Faith Gudgeon – *Sweetbread Croutes*

Cissie Turnbull – *Buttered Fudge (what else?)*

Mr Belvedere – *Brain Fritters*

Dora Dabbs – *Oatmeal Scramble*

Everard – *Feather Pudding*

Apricot Lil – *Apricot Rice*

And, of course, my upside-down cake.

Slack made a wonderful confetti mould, but it wobbled off the plate as she was walking up the church path. I don't think that the Mayoress would have got round to tasting it anyway, because by the time she had tasted the first dozen dishes, she started to go a bit green round the gills, and even worse, her chain of office had dipped into every dish, and I think she was very pleased when her brother turned up with his motorbike and sidecar and whisked her back to the town hall. But there was a winner, Faith Gudgeon and her sweetbread croutes. But of course she didn't claim her prize, because as she said, 'The pew is very nice, but being as I'm always playing the organ anyway, I can't have my behind on two seats at once.'

Well, I didn't say anything, but I knew what she meant by being in two places at once, because I had promised Everard that I would help him cut the top off his climbing ivy, but I'd completely forgotten that I was due to go away with a show called *Tiddle your Wink*.

And, of course, Everard was most upset. But as I said to him, 'Everard, you'll have to learn to do some things on your own, I won't always be here to hold your ladder. Look at Jack and the beanstalk, he didn't have anyone helping him up, and his beanstalk was taller than your ivy! You know your trouble? You always make hard work of everything. Look at Slack Alice, she completely re-arranged her air-raid shelter in one day, and it takes you all the morning to make your own bed! And when you lost your brooch that time while you were washing up, it took you all day to unblock your sink, and goodness knows what you did with my sink plunger, it's got no suck now. Honestly, Everard, sometimes you get right on the end of my tether, it's no wonder your Sunday School mistress finished up with bad nerves. With people like you I'm not surprised!'

Anyway, he could tell I was annoyed, and the next morning he called around with a sweetener, two of his pork and apple dumplings for me to eat on the train. Now, how could I be cross after that? They're guaranteed to keep anyone sweet.

Pork and Apple Dumplings

4 large sour apples
some left-over cooked pork
2 tablespoons breadcrumbs
3 oz grated cheese
salt and pepper
a taste vegetable extract
12 oz shortcrust pastry

Peel and core the apples. Scoop out ¾ of each apple, and keep. Chop the removed portions, and mix with the small pieces of pork, then add the breadcrumbs, grated cheese and seasoning, and blend with the vegetable extract that has been dissolved in a little water.

Fill the hollow apples with the mixture, and roll up in the pastry to make the dumplings.

Bake in a moderate oven for 30–40 minutes, or until the apple is tender.

FRED AND ADA

Well, those dumplings certainly made my journey, and it wasn't until the last week of the tour that I tasted anything nearly as good. And then I happened to get digs with a very dear old couple, namely Fred and Ada Hinch. Yes, I can see their cottage now, thatched roof, cobbled floors, and my own bedroom at the back with a photograph of Lord Kitchener over the washstand and Queen Victoria over the bed. I lay there one night thinking 'I wonder if they ever stayed here.'

I remember that Fred and Ada were still waiting up for me when I came home from the theatre that first night. Fred was sitting shelling peas with his overcoat on, and Ada was sitting in front of the fire quietly playing 'Abide With Me' on her tin whistle, her eyes glazed and her feet resting on top of the cat. And I remember the second night too. Fred was still shelling peas, and Ada was still playing 'Abide With Me', and I remember the cat looking up at me and shrugging its shoulders, as much as to say 'It's the only tune she knows.'

But to give Ada her due she did know about cooking. Not that they bothered much themselves because they were quite content with their pea soup, and as Ada said, 'Fred is ninety-two next month and he enjoys shelling peas because it's the only pleasure he gets, so why spoil it?'

'Ada,' I said, 'if it keeps him young, then why not? After all, if he has the energy to sit up all night shelling peas, who are we to say he's wrong?'

But I must admit they did me proud, and I suddenly felt better than I'd felt for months. I thought, I must go around and see Dr Tizzard when I get back and show him how I can nearly touch my toes again. And I must take back a couple of Ada's recipes for Slack and Everard. Although it was very difficult to choose the dishes I had enjoyed the most. But eventually I settled on two, and here they are.

Country Batter Pie

3 carrots	6 oz steak
2 onions	seasoning
1 lb potatoes	meat or vegetable extract (optional)
½ swede	½ pint batter

Prepare the vegetables in the usual way and cut into cubes. Wipe the meat and cut into small even-sized pieces.

Stew the meat and vegetables together until nearly cooked, but cook in as little liquid as possible. If you want, add some meat or vegetable extract for flavour, and then place the stew into a greased pie dish, pour over the batter, and place into a hot oven.

Cook for about 20–30 minutes.

Ada's Cottage Pudding

2 tablespoons sugar	1 tablespoon margarine
1 teacup flour	1 well-beaten egg
½ teaspoon baking powder	½ teacup milk
½ teaspoon spice	4 stewed apples

Mix the dry ingredients, rub in the margarine and beat in the milk and egg.

Place the stewed apples in the bottom of a greased pie dish, then pour the mixture over.

Bake in a hot oven for about 20 minutes, then sift a little sugar over before serving.

I was going to put in Fred's recipe for pea soup, but I think we can give that a miss.

THE NIGHT THE ROOF BLEW OFF

Well it was a good thing I had built myself up that week, because no sooner had I arrived home, put the kettle on and my washing in the gas boiler, than Slack Alice was rattling my back door like a maniac.

'Slack,' I said, 'give me a chance, I've only been in ten minutes and I'm dying for a brew of selected tips.'

'Laz,' she said, 'brace yourself for a shock.'

'Don't tell me Everard fell off of the ladder!' I said.

'No,' she said, 'but something else fell on Thursday night. They dropped a bomb on the Gem and it blew the roof off.'

'Never!' I said. 'What a blow for the town! Was anybody hurt?'

'No,' she said, 'Lil and Percy should have been up on the roof firewatching, but they had taken two quarts of brown ale up into the projection room and Lil was helping him to unwind. Lil said that after the blast, Percy's pipes were a little bit twisted, but his projector seemed alright, so that was a blessing. But it's no good us trying to show films without a roof, because we've had terrible weather lately, and nobody's going to want to sit there watching *Mrs Miniver* with the rain trickling down the backs of their necks.'

'Slack,' I said, 'surely they can find most of the roof and put it back?'

'No,' she said, 'it's scattered all over the town, and the council say they can't help us anyway, because they've only got one man spare at the moment and he's afraid of heights. And anyway, Percy decided to check the projector yesterday, and after he'd taken it all to bits and put it back together again he had seven bits left over, and nobody knows where they go. So he's in a right old state at the moment and so is Lil, because now that the Gem's closed none of us is getting any wages, and it's messed up all their plans to get married, and they'd already put up the banns and were gearing themselves for the big day. Lil says she doesn't think she can go on much longer with the bedroom wall separating them, and Percy feels the same way, but they've both got high principles because she's C of E and he's a lapsed Methodist, so they've got to stay as they are.'

'Slack,' I said, 'if it's a question of money, they could have a quiet wedding. They don't have to go mad, and I'm sure the Vicar would perform the ceremony at cost if he was asked nicely. I mean, it's no skin off *his* nose, and I should think he'd be pleased for the opportunity to see a few people in church. He's forever moaning about it, and we could all muck in with the food, and you've got enough elderberry wine in your pantry to float a battleship, to say nothing of what you've got tucked away in your air-raid shelter, and Everard has just found a new friend who makes tea wine and mead, so I don't see any problems. Anyway, I'll have a word with the Vicar this afternoon, and then I'll go round to Lil's and see if I can put her mind at rest.'

Well, later that afternoon I called around at the vicarage, and there was the Vicar in the garden tending his hollihocks. 'Vicar,' I said, 'what a grand showing! You could win prizes with those. Let me have a word with our milkman, Sterilised Stan, his horse provides the finest manure for miles. With your green fingers and his manure you could be a world beater. Tell me, how are the attendances going?'

'Lawrence,' he said gravely, 'I feel there is something wrong, I just don't seem to be able to pull them in. I've tried almost everything – free tea and biscuits, and a maximum of sixpence on the collecting plate, and I've even asked Miss Gudgeon to put a bit more sparkle into her organ playing. In fact last Sunday she let herself go with "Kitten on the Keys" but even that didn't seem to attract the masses. In fact, I'm thinking of asking her to step down, because a new lady organist has just moved into the parish. Her name is Maud Moxby, she's a retired cinema organiste, and she has one of those organs that lights up as it rises from the deep.'

'Vicar,' I said, 'what a novelty! There can't be many of those in these parts. What a crowd puller that could be!'

'Yes,' he said. 'The Bishop's already shown an interest.'

'All you need now is a wedding to try her out,' I said. 'Does she know "In the Mood" or even "Roll Me Over in the Clover, Lay Me Down and Do It Again"? It might be a bit more uplifting than "Rock of Ages".

Anyway,' I said, 'The reason I've come to talk to you is that some very dear friends of mine would like to be married next Saturday, but they are a bit short of funds at the moment. Do you think you could waive the charge and call it a try-out? Word would soon spread, you know, and it could be the making of St Agatha's. With every wedding you could put your name down for the christenings.'

'Yes,' he said, 'you're quite right and I shall be pleased to join your friends together in matrimony, but I shall have to make a small charge for the choir.'

'Vicar,' I said, 'don't bother them. I'll get my good friend Everard Farquharson to sing a solo. If his voice is still high enough, he'll do "Oh Perfect Love", and if not, I'm sure they wouldn't object to "Ol' Man River", but we'll see how it goes. I'll just go and tell everyone the good news, then I'll pop back and help you fold up your frontals and polish your pulpit.'

Well of course Lil was over the moon when I told her, and the first thing she did was to pop out into the kitchen and bring me back four fritters on a plate.

'Lawrence,' she said, 'please accept these as a token of my friendship, and if you don't want to eat them now, then please take them for later. Don't worry, I can always make some more.'

'Lil,' I said, 'I can't leave you fritterless, you have them, they'll sustain you in the busy week ahead, and remember to give your legs a rest the day before the wedding. You don't want to be standing at the altar with the backs of your legs playing up. Now then, have a lie down and gather your thoughts while I go around and tell Slack the good news. She's waited for years for a chance to be a maid of honour, and now thanks to you and Percy her dreams have come true.'

'Yes,' Lil said, 'and we would be delighted if you would do us the honour of being the best man.'

'Lil,' I said. 'Of course I will. But I shan't sleep a wink tonight with the thrill of it all. Who's the lucky man that's giving you away?'

'Oh,' she said, 'Mr Pringle, the manager at the Gem.'

'Marvellous,' I said, 'you're obviously well thought of there, and if Slack ever packs it in I wouldn't be surprised if they made you chief usherette. Good luck to you.'

THE WEDDING

Well, everyone was delighted, and we all chipped in and did our bit, and I must say that the wedding went like a dream. Lil walked down the aisle like a queen, and Slack never tripped up once, and you could tell by the look on the Vicar's face that he was pleased to have such a good house. The only pity was that Maud Moxby couldn't perform on her rising organ, because she was all electric and the Vicar was only on gas, so someone had to pump for Faith Gudgeon at the last moment, and it was back to 'Rock of Ages' again.

But to her credit, she did a wonderful job accompanying Everard in 'Oh Perfect Love', and only someone with a very good ear would have realised that he was singing in a different key to her, because she put on her best smile, did a lot of twiddly bits, and put her feet down hard on the loud pedals.

Anyway, Everard eventually twigged what was going on, and finished up just standing there moving his lips. Still, he made up for it later at the reception which was held in the upstairs room at the Cock and Trumpet, and when he sang 'Blessed are the Weary' and 'The Little Boy that Santa Claus Forgot' there was hardly a dry eye in the place. But of course he soon got them all going again, when he got hold of Slack and dragged her on to the floor for a Spasm Dance. I hadn't seen that for many a year, and halfway through I thought Slack was going to have a seizure, but she got into the spirit of it, and after that it was a job to get her off the floor.

The outstanding thing about the day was how everyone contributed with the food, and although Lil's wedding cake was a sponge iced over, the rest of the food was almost pre-war. And I thought at the time, I'll make a note of the recipes, just to show people what could be done at a wartime wedding when people pooled their rations. Here are some of the delights we enjoyed that day.

Cheese Straws

3 oz flour
2 oz breadcrumbs
2 oz grated cheese
2 oz margarine
1 teaspoon water
salt and pepper

Mix ingredients into a stiff paste.

Roll out thinly. Cut into narrow strips, then bake on a greased tin in a hot oven for 10–15 minutes.

Yes, Everard made these. Now I don't know how many people he thought were going to be at the reception, but at the end of the evening I took home half a carrier-bagful, and I was still eating them the following Wednesday!

Then there were the honey rusks that the Vicar made, and he must have spent hours over his hot stove. But they made his day, and I've never seen anyone look so proud as he pushed them around on his kitchen trolley.

The Vicar's Honey Rusks

3 oz margarine
1 oz caster sugar
2 oz honey
grated rind of 1 lemon
8 oz flour
1 teaspoon cream of tartar
$\frac{1}{2}$ teaspoon bicarbonate of soda

Cream the margarine, sugar, honey and lemon rind. Then add the flour, cream of tartar, and bicarbonate of soda, and work into a lump with the hand.

Roll out the mixture on to a floured board until $\frac{1}{2}$ inch thick, and cut into small squares. Bake on a greased tray in a moderate oven until golden brown.

And of course no wedding would be complete without the following.

Confetti Mould

1 lime jelly
water
a few marshmallow sweets
2 glacé cherries
a few chopped nuts

Dissolve the jelly in sufficient water to make up 1 pint. Divide into half. To one half add the sweets cut into small pieces, plus the chopped cherries and nuts. Pour into a wetted mould and allow to set.

When firm, pour on the remaining clear jelly, and stand it in a cool place to set.

Yes, Slack made three confetti moulds from the same recipe as the one that wobbled off of her plate on the way to the Tickle Your Fancy competition. But this time her moulds didn't have so much wobble and that was a blessing if ever there was one. Everard also likes making confetti moulds, but he always puts in liquorice allsorts; of course he has to be different! Between you and me, I always put in hundreds and thousands.

But getting back to the delights, one of the tastiest dishes was provided by the people at the Cock and Trumpet, and it was jumped upon by all and sundry. It was their famous bean and bacon pie.

Bean and Bacon Pie

8 oz haricot beans
2 pints stock
2 oz tapioca, soaked for one hour
salt to taste
1 onion, finely chopped
4 oz fat bacon
pastry

Wash the beans and soak them overnight in the stock. Strain off the stock, and when it is boiling, add the beans and onions. Boil slowly for 45 minutes, then add salt. Place in a greased pie dish with the soaked tapioca and bacon cut into small pieces. Cover with pastry, and bake in a moderate oven for 30–45 minutes.

And of course there were all the wedding presents, although it was difficult to know what to get them, because Lil had most things that she needed in the house, and linen and towels etc were on coupons. But she did get a few useful items, such as:

A musical toilet-roll holder
A gas iron
A lawnmower sharpener
A large framed photograph of Blackpool Tower
A set of fish knives and forks (one fork missing)
Three pre-War paint brushes
A trouser press and assorted coat hangers (some from very posh hotels)
A scout knife (always useful)
A hand-painted egg-timer

Slack also gave her the new ironing board that Maud couldn't take with her, and Everard and I at last got rid of the genuine plaster model of the Alsatian, which we felt might look very nice standing in her front window.

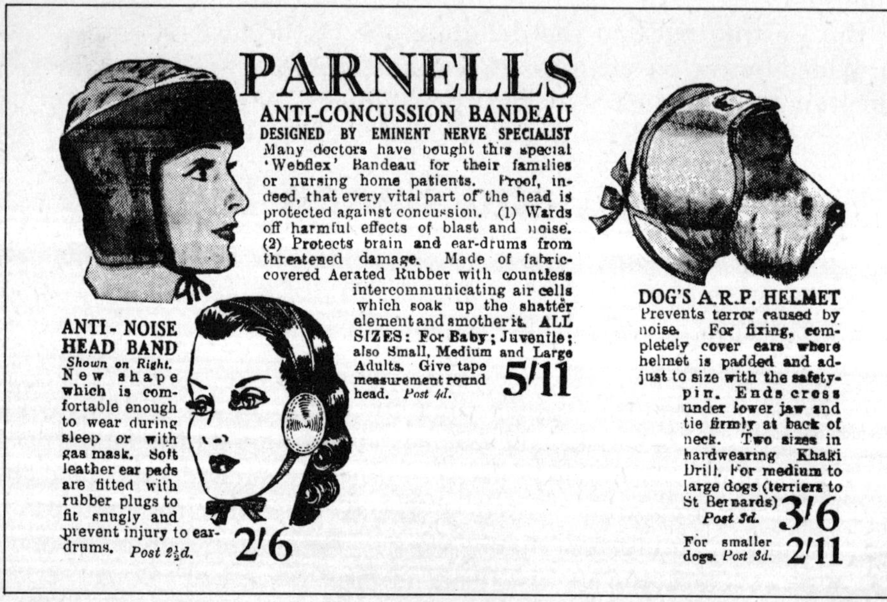

PINEAPPLE PETE

But they didn't have much time to thank us all, because they had to dash away on their honeymoon. Well, I say honeymoon, but they were just having three days in Bolsover, then they had to come back because Percy was due to have two teeth out, and Lil had an appointment to have her ears syringed.

But we all stayed and danced the night away until the drink ran out at about half-past seven. And what a good day it had been, and what a treat to see Slack up on the floor dancing again after all these years. And it suddenly reminded me of the time before the war when she had a crush on another local bandleader – Pineapple Pete and his Pearldivers. I always remember him because he had the biggest feet I've ever seen. Slack said that was probably because where he came from they didn't wear shoes and his feet had spread, but she was in a lover's trance and I have a suspicion the last thing she was thinking about was his feet.

You see, it all started one night when he picked her out twice in a spot waltz, and she'd never been picked out before. And afterwards she said that he'd been looking at her all night with a glint in his eye, and Slack never forgot him. In fact, a couple of days after Lil's wedding, Slack said to me, 'Laz, I wonder if Pineapple Pete ever went back to his island in the sun? I shall never forget how he used to look at me.'

Well, I just couldn't answer her. How could I tell her, after all these years, that his real name was Fred Crutchin, that he was a steamboiler welder, and he had a glass eye? How could I destroy a dream?

I know for a fact that Slack went home still thinking about him, because she made one of her pineapple puddings, and brought me some round that evening. That's what dreams are made of, I suppose.

Slack's Pineapple Pudding

1 tin pineapple
4 oz flour
4 oz breadcrumbs
4 oz sugar
1½ tablespoons cocoa
1½ teaspoons baking powder
pinch salt
3 oz margarine
2 eggs
4–6 tablespoons milk

Cut the pineapple into small pieces. Put the sieved flour, breadcrumbs, sugar, cocoa, and baking powder into a basin with a pinch of salt and half of the chopped pineapple, reserving the other half for a sauce. Rub in the margarine, then add the beaten eggs and enough milk to make a fairly stiff mixture. Pour into a well-buttered pudding basin, cover with greased paper and steam for 2 hours.

The pineapple sauce is an ordinary sweet white sauce to which the other half of the chopped pineapple has been added.

— ROBINSON CRUSOE —

Shortly after the wedding I went away for a couple of months in pantomime, and that was a big mistake, I can tell you! The show was called *Robinson Crusoe Meets Girl Friday* and as soon as I arrived at the first rehearsal I knew something was amiss, because there were only two people there, a large man smoking a cigar, and a large lady, plus one goat. I said to the man, 'Excuse me, but I thought there was to be a rehearsal here for *Robinson Crusoe Meets Girl Friday*.'

He said. 'Yes, this is it, you're Robinson Crusoe and this is Bessie Babcock, who is playing Girl Friday.'

Girl!! She was seventy if she was a day! I said, 'Surely there must be others in the cast?'

'Yes,' he said. 'There's the goat, and we're trying to get hold of a cockatoo. You see, owing to the war we've had to cut out a lot of the big scenes, so in a way this is a utility pantomime.'

'Well,' I said, 'I'm aghast. I'm used to bigger things, even with my Strolling Players we had more than this. In fact, in our dramatic play *The Night Her Candle Blew Out* there were four of us under the bed, three in the wardrobe and two trying to get up the chimney. So you see I'm used to working with a big cast.'

But it was no good trying to talk to him. The show opened a few days later and what a disaster it was.

Well, I stuck it out for a couple of nights, and then I went to see him straight after the curtain had come down.

'Oscar,' I said, 'I'm the last person in the world to complain, but something must be done about that woman. She has no sense of direction on or off the stage and is forever standing on my foot. And you know how heavy she is, if she goes on like this I shall finish up having to play my part in a wheelchair. And not only that, but tonight in our big dramatic scene where we're down to our last coconut, she bent down to pick it up and her teeth dropped out! And it wouldn't go amiss either if you were to lay out some money on proper stage make-up for

her. It takes her hours to rub herself all over with that cocoa and boot-polish mixture, and then when she comes on the goat is forever licking her! And when it's not licking *her* it's always chewing something else. It had me on that bamboo mat three times tonight. For goodness sake give it something to eat before it comes on, or better still, write in another scene where we eat the goat.'

'No way,' he said flatly. 'At the moment the goat is getting more laughs than you are, so the goat stays.'

'Well,' I said, 'Couldn't you at least make my bamboo hut a little bigger? There just isn't room for that woman and me. Every time she comes in I get pushed out through the back window.'

'Yes,' he said, 'I was going to mention that. Tonight when you came through the window you screamed. Keep it in, it's a good dramatic effect.'

All through our childhood there was magic in these words. As we grew older "the holidays" were looked forward to throughout the working year.

But today . . . the German armies have over-run half Europe. Thousands have fled from their bombed and burning homes. Invasion threatens our Island. We must put aside all thought of going away for holidays until this war is over and victory is won.

So let us speed up our war effort. Let us lend our "holiday money" to the Nation. Put every shilling into National Savings (Savings Certificates, Defence Bonds, National War Bonds, Post Office and Trustee Savings Banks). The money is urgently needed to pay for the equipment of our fighting forces — for the defence of our shores, our homes, our lives.

This year make your holiday weeks National Savings Weeks!

Issued by the National Savings Committee, London

— THE CONTORTIONIST —

Well, how I stuck it out I shall never know, and the only thing that kept me sane was the fact that I had wonderful theatrical digs, and that saw me through.

You see, I was staying with a very dear old friend of pre-war days, Winifred Brinsmead. And what a wonderful woman she was! She was double jointed, and for years before the war she had toured the music halls as a contortionist, and even at the age of seventy-three could still bend over backwards, put her head between her legs and whistle 'Mother McCree'.

'Winn,' I used to say, 'you certainly haven't lost your touch, I don't know how you do it. I only have to lift up my leg to put a sock on and I go dizzy, and what Slack Alice would give to be as agile as you. Tell me, what is the secret?'

'Well,' she said, 'I had a wonderful husband, and every night before we went to bed he would think up a new position for me, and he wouldn't turn out the light until I had got it right.'

'Winn,' I said, 'he must have been devoted to you. How many men would take the trouble to do that?'

'Yes,' she said, 'and sometimes if it was particularly difficult he used to applaud.'

'Winn,' I said, 'what a happy life you must have led, doing something you enjoyed, and giving pleasure to the masses. I remember seeing you at the old Hippodrome when you used to tie yourself in a knot and invite members of the audience up to try to untie you. What a finale that was, and they could never unravel you.'

'No, never,' she said, 'but now I can tell you the secret. What they never realised was that the first thing they had to do was ease my foot out of my mouth, then everything else followed. But they always went for the other bits, and all they did was to pull the knot tighter together.'

'Well,' I said, 'it just goes to show there's an art in everything, and it's just as well you had your foot in your mouth, otherwise some nights I'm sure you would have doubled up with laughter. But what a clever act you had. Do you know, some people tend to forget that you were the first person in this country to wrap yourself around a totem pole like a corkscrew while at the same time singing a selection from *Rose Marie*.'

'Yes,' she said, 'but I couldn't do it now, I've completely forgotten the words.'

Well, of course, Winn was one of the best, and we shall never see her like again. She looked after me like a mother all those weeks, and if I ever had one of my turns she was always there with a comforting word, and in spite of the rationing she always kept a good table.

The very last day I was there, she pulled out all the stops, and we sat down to our farewell supper.

'Winn,' I said, 'you've done us proud, and I shall always treasure these memories.'

And this is what we sat down to on my last evening with her.

Confused British troops prepare to invade Brighton.

Winn's Rabbit Croquettes

½ oz dripping
1 small onion
½ oz flour
¼ pint stock
pinch dried herbs
8 oz finely minced rabbit
2 finely chopped streaky rashers
1 egg
salt and pepper
breadcrumbs
1 teaspoon chopped parsley

Melt the dripping in a saucepan, then stir in the chopped onion and fry till golden brown. Then remove onions from the saucepan and stir in the flour. Lower the heat and cook very slowly until the flour is evenly browned.

Add the stock, and stir while it is coming to the boil. Then add the finely chopped onion, herbs, meat and rashers, and beat well to blend the mixture, then stir in enough egg to bind. Season.

Turn out on to a plate, spread out evenly, and allow to cool.

Divide into ten pieces of even size. Flour a board and shape each portion into a flat cake or ball. Brush over with beaten egg, coat with breadcrumbs, then place in a frying basket and fry in the normal way until golden brown. And of course they can also be fried in shallow fat. Serve garnished with parsley.

I can tell you, I slept like a log that night and it's just as well, because I never realised what a busy day I would have when the next day came.

A SEIZE-UP IN WORKSOP

Yes, I was up bright and early, and I'd just finished packing my holdall when Winn came in to say that there were no trains running from the station because there had been an air raid during the night, and one of the bridges down the line had been hit. Well, I was in a state of flux.

'What ever shall I do?' I asked. 'I have to get back, I have an appointment with Dr Tizzard. He wanted to see me before I came away but I had to put him off.'

'Well,' she said, 'you can always hitch-hike.'

'Winn,' I said, 'I haven't hitched my hike for years, I wouldn't know where to begin.'

'Well, the best place to start,' she said, 'is at the side of the road. Just point your thumb and take pot luck.'

'Winn, that's the story of my life', I said. 'But you're right, and if I don't get a lift straightaway I shall start to walk. After all, Dick Whittington did it, so why can't I?'

Just two hours later, there I was at the side of the road looking like a lost soul. All that had passed by was a herd of cows, a vicar on a bicycle, and an old lady pushing a pram full of firewood.

Then suddenly, a shy retiring Army dispatch rider pulled up on his motorcycle. 'Hop on,' he cried, 'I'm sure I'm going your way.' And he was.

Hey ho, up hill, down dale. What a gay day, I thought. I haven't gone as fast as this since the day that Everard and I were cycling down to Monks Bottom on the tandem and the brakes failed. But of course I should have realised that things were going too well, and lo and behold, just as we were passing through Worksop the engine seized up.

Well, the first thing I did was to phone Dr Tizzard. 'Doctor,' I said when I'd pressed Button A, 'I've just had a breakdown in Worksop.'

'That's not unusual,' he said. 'Try and get a grip on yourself, take a sedative and come and see me as soon as possible. Tell me, have you been crying yet?'

'No,' I said.

'You will,' he replied. 'You will.'

'Doctor,' I said, 'I think you've got the wrong end of the stick, I haven't had a *nervous* breakdown but I've been travelling with a friend and he's just seized up.'

'Not to worry,' he said, 'I know Worksop well. There's a little café at the back of the abattoir, go there and order yourself a large portion of Worksop hotpot. It'll make you feel like a new man.' That's the best suggestion so far, I thought. At least it's a step in the right direction.

Anyway, I found the café, it was called The Trusting Chef, which was a strange name I thought, especially as the only teaspoon was on a chain, and all the tablecloths were nailed down. But they did serve a delicious hotpot, and so I asked if I could have the recipe.

Well, I think the chef must have been foreign, because here is the recipe which I had to translate from the original Swahili.

Worksop Hotpot

½ neck mutton
2 kidneys
8 oz sausagemeat
seasoning
small bunch herbs
water or stock
3 large onions
1 lb potatoes

Cut the mutton into joints and remove some of the fat. Cut the kidneys and remove the core, and cut the sausagemeat into squares.

Place the mutton, kidney and sausagemeat in the bottom of a pie dish, then add the seasoning and herbs, and cover with water or stock.

Add a layer of sliced onions, and arrange peeled and sliced potatoes on top. Cover with greased paper, and cook slowly in a moderate oven for about 2 hours. Remove the paper a short while before serving, so that the potatoes have a chance to brown.

A VISIT TO THE DOCTOR

Well, eventually I did get home, and the first thing I did was to call on Dr Tizzard. 'Doctor,' I said, 'that hotpot certainly did the trick. In fact I feel so well I don't really know what I'm doing here.'

'Lawrence,' he said, 'it's just as well to have a check-up every now and again. Tell me, have you had any problems over the last few months, and if not, why not?'

'I did have a couple of problems while I was away in pantomime,' I told him. 'Every night a big woman stood on my feet, and I had trouble with a goat that would keep nibbling, but apart from that I've been in the pink. Except for my usual little things, like feeling as faint as a robin when I lift my head from the pillow in the morning, and I still keep going limp when there's an "r" in the month, but I've lived with that for years. It doesn't affect me socially, I still mingle.'

'Lawrence,' he said, 'you sound as if you're almost back to your normal health. Keep up the good work, but do come and see me from time to time, because I haven't been feeling all that well lately, and it's nice to have a chat with a friend when you've spent most of the night lying awake looking up at the ceiling hoping the throbbing will stop.'

'Doctor,' I said, 'anytime you're feeling under the weather and need to have a chat, you know where I live, that's what friends are for – to give a comforting word or maybe share a joke. Don't worry, why don't you close up now and have a tablet and a lie down? You'll feel alright again after a little doze.'

'Yes,' he said, 'maybe you're right. I have been overdoing it, and another thing, I've been reading so many books lately on diseases and their symptoms that I'm beginning to imagine that I've got every illness under the sun.'

'It's easily done,' I said. 'I remember Everard reading a book on dogs once, and it took the vet three months to convince him that he didn't have hardpad. Come along, doctor, settle yourself down and I'll call and see you when you're better. Meanwhile, I'm just going to pop round to see my dear friends Lil and Percy, and see how married life is treating them.'

The 'Shy Retiring Dispatch Rider' having a drink of Perrier water after our arrival in Worksop.

THE GRAND REOPENING

Well, I knocked on Lil's door, and after a while she opened it; but I could hardly believe my eyes.

'Lil,' I said, 'what a difference in one person. Marriage is obviously doing wonders for you, your cheeks are rosy and your eyes are positively sparkling.'

'Yes,' she said, 'but that's because I've been standing over a steamed pudding peeling onions.'

'Never mind,' I said, 'you're looking well. I remember the time when you used to come to the front door looking as if you'd just been through the mangle backwards. Compared with that you're looking radiant.'

'Yes,' she said, 'I must admit that married life has given me a lift, and I don't shout as much since I had my ears syringed. And I can hear everything so clearly now, especially at night. In fact, when Percy and I are in bed, I can even hear his heavy breathing.'

'Lil,' I said, 'don't give all your secrets away!'

'No,' she said, 'I mean he's a bit bronchial.'

'Ah,' I said, 'but you've got to remember he's a married man now, with a lot on his chest. Tell me, how are things at the Gem?'

'Well,' she said, 'they managed to find someone to repair the roof, and we opened again last Monday. We had a special double bill with *The Man who Came to Dinner*, followed by *Goodbye Mr Chips*, and that gave the manager a good idea. So after the show we put on a buffet supper for selected patrons, although it wasn't really a buffet supper because we only had sausages and baked beans with soft rolls, and the sausages weren't anything to write home about. In the event they were served on thin paper plates, and as the plates sagged most people's sausages fell on the floor anyway. In fact, the only thing that took our minds off the food was Ada Gringle and her Palm Court Trio playing in front of the box office. A few people tried to dance but it didn't come to anything because Ada had only brought along her selections from *The Desert Song* and *Madam Butterfly* so after a few steps most people gave up and went home, but at least it was different, I suppose.'

"Well,' I said, 'in a way I'm glad I missed it, although I've always admired Ada Gringle's violin playing, and when Cissie Nottle used to play "The Swan" on her cello I used to go cold all over.'

'Yes,' she said, 'and they didn't come cheap. The manager had to pay them a pound each, and they only played for about twenty minutes.'

'What's money on an occasion like that?' I said. 'And although it may not have been the event of the year, at least it'll be talked about, and you're all back at work and that's a blessing.'

'Right,' she said, 'but things are still a bit topsy-turvy, and Percy's pipes are still a bit twisted, and that's doing him no good at all. When he's up there in the projection room the bottom half of him is warm and the top half of him is cold, and it meets somewhere around his navel, so it's no wonder he's a bit bronchial!'

'Lil,' I said, 'what he needs is a liberty bodice, I'll see if I can pick him up one the next time I go to a jumble sale. Meanwhile, I'm going to pop around and see Slack, I should think she's thrilled about the Gem being open again. Give my regards to Percy, and buy him a jar of Vick.'

Well, of course, when I saw Slack she was over the moon about the Gem. 'Laz,' she said, 'I haven't been so thrilled since my marrow was blessed, and that's a while ago now.'

'And a lot of water has passed under your bridge since then, Slack,' I said. 'But you've always kept your chin up high and taken everything in your stride and now the Gem is open again you'll be playing your part in taking people's minds off the war as you lead them down to their seats and leave them to enjoy a couple of hours in the dark. By the way, what are you showing next week?'

'*Hell's Angels* and *The Battle of Alamein*', she replied, 'but there's a cartoon and adverts too. How things have changed since the days of Shirley Temple and the Lone Ranger, and the days when Maud had an overpowering urge to mother that nice Wallace Beery.'

'Slack,' I said, 'how is dear Maud? Have you heard from her recently?'

'Yes,' she said, 'I had a nice long letter from her just last week, and she seems very contented with life in general. She says that she and her gentleman friend have been practising a lot of new numbers, and now they go around at weekends entertaining the old age pensioners, which is very nice, I'm sure. She says her gentleman is a dab-hand on his banjo now, and he always gets a lot of applause when he stops. She told me that they were a bit disappointed the other week, though, because they went to one of the local hospitals and asked the matron if she would like them to play for the patients. The matron said that she didn't feel that the patients were strong enough for that at the moment, but she'd keep them in mind and let them know. But one thing that Maud is really excited about is they're thinking of forming a little concert party. She says that they know a lovely lady singer who does things like "Bless This House" and "Jerusalem" and a bit of comedy too if required. And they've got their eye on a ventriloquist. Maud says that he isn't all that good because his lips move all the time, but the dummy is very funny. And they're also interested in a magician, but they're having a bit of a job to pin him down, because he keeps on disappearing. But Maud says that she's sure they'll be able to make a go of it, and she's already thinking of putting their name down to do a *Worker's Playtime* on the wireless.

'Slack,' I said, 'that could be the making of them. Imagine the thrill of switching on and hearing Maud playing, and saying to people, "I knew her when she used to trip up and down the aisle at the Gem". Yes, the war has certainly changed our lives, Slack, but come and have a bite of lunch with me. I was going to invite Everard, but he's gone to visit the Vicar.'

'I'd be delighted to join you, Laz,' she said. 'What have you got?'

'Well,' I said, 'I'm trying out a recipe that was given to me by a dear old lady I met before the war in a tiny village in Norfolk. She was an amazing hundred and two years old, and was kindness itself. She used to look after ducks that had bad feet. The only trouble was, they used to follow her everywhere she went, and they usually finished up with worse feet than when they first started, and her feet weren't all that clever either, but what a lovely lady, I wonder if she's still about? Anyway, she gave me the recipe one day after I'd helped her lift her pigs over the fence – they were anxious to get on the other side – and I remember as I helped her up off her knees she said, "You shall have my recipe for long life, it was given to me by my mother who was an American, and who would have been alive today if she hadn't been trampled on by a herd of wild buffalo whilst crossing the street. Please take it as a memento from a very grateful old lady."'

Well, of course, Slack was near to tears when I'd finished the story, but she soon came round, and within a short while we were sitting down to that very same recipe that the old lady had given me all those years ago – hash à la mode.

Hash à la Mode

½ pint white sauce	a little milk
finely grated horseradish	8 oz corned beef
6 medium-sized potatoes	3 oz stale cheese

Prepare a white sauce of medium thickness, then add the finely grated horseradish.

Mash the potatoes with a little milk, and line a greased pie dish with them, but keep some for the top.

Cut the beef into neat pieces, and place in the pie dish. Add the sauce and horseradish, and cover the top with the rest of the mashed potato.

Sprinkle with cheese, and put in a hot oven to brown and heat thoroughly.

BRENDA ALCOCK

Well, after we had eaten and were relaxing with a cup of lemon tea and a cavendish cake, Slack turned to me and said, 'Laz, you'll never guess who I saw outside the seed shop this morning – Brenda Alcock.'

'Never!' I said. 'Not Big Brenda! I never thought she'd show her face back here again, not after all that trouble there was over that under-manager at the Home and Colonial, and then that gas fitter from Jasmine Street. Do you remember! I don't know how she can hold her head up, especially after swanking that she'd been offered a *pied-à-terre* in the better part of Paddington, and was thinking of taking up modelling. And who believed that! For a start her feet were too big, and every time you talked to her you always felt she was looking over your shoulder. Mind you, I blame the mother, she was never any good. She always walked about with bare legs and a big red hat stuck on her head, and I'm sure she never wore a stitch under that fur coat of hers. I remember how her cheeks used to flush as soon as there was the slightest wind. What's more, she was always creeping around Freddie Fillet's father after some choice chunks, and I know for a fact that she never paid for any milk in the old days, because Sterilised Stan himself told me that the milkman who used to be on her round used to give her a free one every weekday and two on Sunday, so you can make up your own mind about that. And I'm sure she never had a husband; if she did she must have kept him locked up in a cupboard because I never saw him and I've always had good eyes. Mind you, she soon disappeared when the war started, and the last thing I heard she was down near Aldershot – enough said.'

Well, of course, Slack knew more about Big Brenda than I did, but she didn't say anything. I think the reason was that they both had a crush on the same person in their younger days – namely, Horace Hodd. He was a violinist who played locally as Horace Hodd, his Violin and his Hot-Shots. Mind you, he never married, and the last I heard of him he had packed up the violin, had started making perfume and was still living with his mother, but I never said anything to Slack. Anyway, after she'd had half an hour asleep in the chair she gathered herself together and toddled off, and I was just about to wash my hair when Everard knocked on my door.

'Everard,' I said, 'I thought you were taking luncheon with the Vicar, and then spending the afternoon together playing cribbage. Didn't you say that he had mentioned something about having kidney twists?'

'Lawrence,' he said, 'that's what I thought, but it was *his* kidneys he was talking about. He thinks he twisted them when he was trying to re-point his weathercock, but he never quite managed it, and now nobody can tell which way the wind is blowing because the weathercock has fallen halfway down the steeple.'

'If people would only leave things as they are,' I said. 'You know my motto, "If a thing is working well, leave it alone."'

'Agreed,' he said, 'but you know the Vicar, he won't be told, and now he's looking for someone to climb up the steeple and replace it.'

'Well, he'll have a long wait. It makes me go dizzy even thinking about it. Meanwhile what are you going to do about eating? You can't go all day without something passing your lips, and I know for a fact that all you've got in your pantry is half a cornish pastie and a tin of sardines. Here, sit down and read *The Camping Times* while I rustle you up a little something.'

Well, this is the little something that I came up with, and although it's not exactly from the menu at the Ritz, at least it filled a gap in wartime.

Economy Fritters

3 slices stale bread
1 tablespoon flour
1 teacup milk
fat for frying
1 tablespoon jam
1 tablespoon sugar

Cut each slice of bread into 4 pieces. Mix the flour and milk into a smooth batter, and soak the bread in it for about 30 minutes.

Melt the fat in the frying pan, and drop the slices of bread in. Fry until golden brown, then drain on paper.

Spread half the slices with jam, and put the other slices on top. Sprinkle a little sugar on top and serve.

Well, no sooner had Everard eaten the last fritter when there came another knock on my knocker. I thought, 'Hello! Who can that be? I shall die if it's Brenda Alcock!' But it wasn't. It was a boy with a telegram for Mr Grayson, and it said, would I like to join a show called *A Little Bit of This, and a Little Bit of That*? It was for a ten-week tour, and to name my own price providing it was under five pounds. Well, I pushed them to the hilt by asking for four pounds, nineteen and sixpence and got the job.

One of Brenda Alcock's first modelling jobs. She's the one who's upside down. What else?

— THE KNIFE-THROWER —

The very next day I set out to meet the show in Rotherham as they were already in the middle of the tour, and I was to take over from the previous comedian who had just had a nervous breakdown. When I saw the show I wasn't surprised!

I can't remember all the acts, but there was a Chinese juggler called Sam Pan, and the Van Winkle Sisters, who did scenes from *The Sleeping Beauty*, and I think they must have been asleep for a few years themselves, because they were always telling everyone how they were coming up to their thirtieth birthday, and they had complexions like leather.

Then there was the knife-thrower and his wife, and his hands were so shaky he could hardly hold a spoon and fork! I remember asking his wife one night after he'd practically pinned her to the board, 'How long have you been doing this act?' 'Three months,' She said, 'and look at the scars on my arms.'

'Vera,' I said, 'think yourself lucky. Have you seen the theatre cat? One of your husband's knives went amiss tonight and they say that it'll never father kittens again. In just three seconds its whole life was changed, and it had only popped in to the wings for a saucer of milk!'

'That's nothing,' she said. 'Last week, after I had blindfolded him, with only four knives he managed to hit the drummer, the lady violinist and a woman who was just coming out of the toilet.'

'I can tell you,' I said, 'I shan't feel safe until this tour is over. Do try and have a word with him in bed, and tomorrow morning make up this recipe for him. It's savoury scrambled egg. I used to have a friend with shaky hands, and at one time he couldn't even lick a postage stamp, but after a couple of days on savoury eggs, not only could he lick the stamps he could seal down the envelope and felt confident enough to go to the postbox on his own. Just try him on this for a week, and your scars will be gone before you know it.'

Well, of course, it was the very same recipe that I made up for

Everard when he went through a stage of self-doubt, and it was one of the things that helped to pull him through.

Savoury Scrambled Egg

1 egg
½ oz margarine
2 tablespoons milk
1 tomato
1 tablespoon chopped ham or cold meat
½ teaspoon chopped parsley
1½ tablespoons breadcrumbs
salt and pepper
2 slices buttered toast

Scramble the egg with the margarine and milk. Then add the sliced tomato, chopped meat, parsley and breadcrumbs. Season.

Place on top of the toast, and stand back for the applause.

I'm pleased to say that my savoury scrambled egg did the trick for our knife-thrower, and apart from one little incident which involved the Chinese juggler, three goldfish and the lady violinist, who always played with her mouth open, the show went almost without a hitch.

Mind you, I was lucky again with my digs, and if it hadn't been for those it might have been a different story.

— AT CISSIE HODGE'S —

You see, whatever show you were in – good, bad or indifferent – you always knew that you were going back to the comfort and bonhomie of your digs, and at Cissie Hodge's you always knew that you were going back to something hot, because she always left a saucepan of soup and a packet of cream crackers for supper, and it always worked out at four crackers each – three dips per cracker.

Yes, I can see us all now, standing around the gas cooker, talking about the events of the day as we all dunked our crackers one by one. Then we'd hear Cissie bang the gong that she kept by the side of her bed, and we knew it was time to light our candles and troop off to bed.

I remember how sometimes I used to lie in bed thinking I wonder whatever happened to Freddie Bartholomew? I wonder if he took up the sea after *Captains Courageous*? And, what a pity they shot Gunga Din, he would have done well if he had lived, he could have appeared in other films as Sabu's father. Yes, all these things used to flit through my mind, and then all of a sudden I'd drop off.

Then, in the morning, we'd hear the cat wake up first. It always had a terrible cough as if it was being strangled. And then there was just time to splash our faces before dashing down to breakfast.

I can see Cissie now, walking in with two frying pans full of porridge – she had some strange ways that woman – and then she would bring in the toast on a hot-water bottle – to keep it warm, she said – then take about ten minutes to find the key to the sideboard where she kept the marmalade. Next came the big moment, when she wheeled in the tea-urn, and we all made a grab for the biggest mug.

And then, after breakfast, Cissie would bring in the morning paper, tear it up so we could all have a page each, and we'd while away the time chatting and swopping pages, and before we knew it, it was half-past eight.

Yes, they were good days, and I remember saying to Cissie, 'Cissie, you certainly run a tight ship, and whenever I stay here I always feel the benefit. My leg hasn't played up once this week, and every night I've slept like a top. If my local vicar ever decides to take a tandem holiday, I'll get him to pass this way. He'd love staying with you, and he could soak in the atmosphere of pure showbusiness. You could tell him about the time you were a bubble-dancer at Skegness, or about the time you did the splits on that sloping stage and finished up with your legs wrapped around the drummer, and how it nearly led to marriage. And the time you were shot out of that cannon and your tights blew off. He'd be interested in that, and it might give him some ideas for his next garden fête. Yes,' I said, 'one day you'll have to write your life story, and I know one thing, if half the things that have happened to you had happened to Slack Alice she would have been a different woman.'

And it's true, because when I got back home there was Slack still plodding down the street in her panda boots and balaclava carrying her gas mask.

'Slack,' I said, 'you'll have to move faster than that. If your tortoise ever comes out of hibernation, he could race you to your front gate and win!'

'Laz,' she said, 'I can't help it, I feel drained. Ever since you've been away I've seemed to get slower and slower. In fact, yesterday morning I had an appointment with Dr Tizzard, and by the time I crawled round there he was closed.'

'Slack,' I said, 'don't let it beat you, there's still a war to be won and the country needs people like you. You may be a plodder, but you always get there in the end. But imagine what you could do if you ever managed to move fast. You'd be unbeatable. What you need is some deep breathing, give your lungs a chance. Don't forget your poem 'Stick it out for Britain'. Well, Slack, stick it out again!'

I think my little pep talk did the trick, because the very next day there she was, out in her garden doing her deep breathing exercises. She was puffing like a steam engine, but I could tell the fresh air was doing her good. She came bouncing over to me full of the joys of spring.

'Laz,' she said, 'that deep breathing is working wonders for me. My mind is as clear as a bell and it's giving me a wonderful appetite. I've been saving a tin of pineapple slices for a special occasion and I feel like opening it, but I'm not going to open it unless you promise to share it with me.'

'Slack,' I said, 'Go and put on your sarong, wind up your gramophone, and we'll have Bing Crosby singing "Song of the Islands" while we eat.'

Well, I shall never forget the pineapple fritters that she made, it was like stumbling across an oasis in the desert, and every mouthful was a banquet.

'Slack,' I said, 'you've surpassed yourself today. These fritters are fit for a king. You must let me have the recipe, and I will tuck it away in my book of memories.'

Well, I've untucked it and here it is once more.

Pineapple Fritters with Pineapple Sauce

1 tin pineapple slices
1 egg
3 oz flour
milk
1 oz cornflour

Drain the pineapple and put the juice into a small saucepan.

Make a batter with the yolk of the egg, flour and milk. Beat well, then whip the white of the egg, and add it to the batter just before using.

Stick the pineapple slices on to a skewer, and dip them into the batter, then fry them.

Mix the cornflour into a paste with a spoonful of water, then add to the pineapple juice. Bring it to the boil, stirring all the time.

Pour it over your fritters, lick your lips, and dive in.

THE LAST STRAWBERRY

When I told Everard about the pineapple fritters he went all strange. 'Oh,' he said. 'How the rich live! Nobody thought of asking me if I would like one, I suppose it all depends on which end of the street you live. But when the Salvation Army Band comes down here they play up this end of the street as well, you know.'

'Everard,' I said, 'what on earth has the Salvation Army got to do with it? Slack just happened to have a tin of pineapple and we shared it, that's all.'

'Yes,' he said, 'I remember giving my last strawberry to a friend once, but it doesn't seem to count for much.'

'Everard,' I said, 'you've been on about that strawberry for years! I'm sorry I took it now. If I'd have known I would have to live with it for all these years I would have left it where it was! You'll be reminding me next about the time you shared that pomegranate with me, and your half was bad. Honestly, I thought you were above things like jealousy, and it's no good standing there with your eyes flashing with temper, you know that doesn't cut any soap with me. Anyway, I'm going to have a lie down now, and when that little green eye of envy leaves you, you're always welcome to pop around and have a cup of tea and a bath bun. I never hold it against any man, as you well know, so snap out of it.'

Well, of course, he came around later that day and was charm itself. 'Lawrence,' he said, 'I'm sorry about this afternoon, and I'm sorry I mentioned the strawberry again, but I just feel as if I'm missing out on life somewhere.'

'Everard,' I said, 'of course you're missing out on life. Look at all the things you used to do at one time, you always had your finger into something, and whatever happened to all your hobbies, like basket weaving and catching newts on a Sunday afternoon down at the pond?

EVERARDS SNACK BAR
OPEN
if you're tired and listles
and the war gets on your wick
then give yourself a special treat
some good old spotted DICK
It's tasty And its good for you
and helps keep out the cold
my Auntie Maggie loves it
and she's Ninety three years old
So if You've used YOUR RATIONS – AND
There's nothing you can roast –
your sausages keep shrivelling – and your
sick of Things on toast – then pull
yourself together – stop feelling life
is flat – Just order up some spotted
Dick – and get your teeth 'round that.

And I haven't seen you pick up your embroidery for months! Honestly, you've got a grasshopper mind, you jump from one thing to another . . . even the Vicar was surprised when you gave up origami after only two lessons. But he stuck it out, and now after he's read the *News of the World* on a Sunday he folds it up and makes all sorts of things.'

'Yes,' he said, 'but I feel my fingers are meant for other things. In fact, I'm seriously thinking of taking over that little snack bar around the corner from the Gem.'

'Bully for you, Everard,' I said. 'That's what you need, something to occupy your day. And think of all the new friends you'll make, you'll get to know the dustmen for a start, and that won't be a bad thing; you're always complaining about how they lost your dustbin lid, and that was five years ago! Maybe they'll find you a new one.'

'Yes,' he said, 'but what I have in mind is a snack bar with a difference, a little refuge where people can savour the unusual, instead of just luncheon meat and pickle sandwiches. I'd like to offer them my little fruity cakes and a selection of savouries on toast fingers, but I'm only going to take it over on two weeks' trial.'

'Everard,' I said, 'I'm sure you'll be on a winner, but choose your menu carefully. In fact, I'll give you a hand and we'll choose the menu together.'

Well, of course, I should have known better, because it finished up with Everard just picking the things he liked. But, as he said, if there was going to be anything left over at the end of the day, he could always have it for supper, and at least he wouldn't have to force down something that he wasn't keen on.

'Look here,' I said, 'I know you like all those titbits, but you'll have to have more than that to entice the locals in. Now then, what is the most popular dish they serve in the British Restaurant? Yes, spotted dick. Always make sure that's on your menu every day, and I don't see how you can go wrong. Slack Alice and Apricot Lil will spread the word in the Gem if you ask them nicely, and then once you're into the big money you could advertise on the screen.'

Well, when I told Slack about Everard's plans she was so thrilled that she sat down that very night and wrote a special verse for him to put in the window. And, of course, it was in praise of spotted dick.

Give Yourself a Special Treat

If you're tired and listless,
And the war 'gets on your wick',
Then give yourself a special treat,
Some good old spotted dick.

It's tasty and it's good for you,
And helps keep out the cold,
My Auntie Maggie loves it,
And she's ninety-three years old.

So, if you've used your rations,
And there's nothing you can roast,
Your sausages keep shrivelling,
And you're sick of things on toast,
Then pull yourself together,
Stop feeling life is flat,
Just order up some spotted dick,
And get your teeth round that.

Well, Slack's verse certainly did the trick, and when Everard took over the snack bar he could hardly keep up with the demand, it seemed the whole world wanted to sample his spotted dick. Of course the snag was he never sold anything else! And every night he used to sit by his fireside eating anchovies on toast, one after the other. In fact, he used to invite us all around to help him eat them. But after a while even we got sick of anchovies.

Slack took a couple of basketsful for Mr Belvedere to take with him for the Home Guard, but after two nights he pushed a note through her letterbox saying they were very nice, but no more thank you!

Well, Everard stuck it out for the couple of weeks, and then decided he'd had enough. I remember him saying, 'Lawrence, although I've actually made some money, I just can't go on. I can't give the rest of my life to spotted dick.'

'Well, at least you've left your mark,' I said. 'Some men climb mountains, others go up the Amazon in a canoe, but you, in your own way, have done something equally as noble, you've put your spotted dick on a pedestal, and no one can take that away from you. Now then, why don't you think about making something special for Christmas? Make a start now and it'll take your mind off the last two weeks, and give you a chance to get rid of the taste of anchovies.'

'Yes,' he said, 'I've already been thinking about it, but I'm not making a Christmas cake this year. Instead, I'm going to make my own mincemeat, and then at Christmas I shall make lots of mince pies and send some to our lads out east and give the rest to the cottage hospital.'

'Everard,' I said, 'what a spendid gesture! Mind you, they've been very good to you at that hospital over the years, and they've always made sure that you had a bed near the window so you could wave to people that were passing. And look how many friends you've made that way over the years. If it hadn't been for that window, you would have never met that all-in wrestler from Tahiti, and you would never have taken up his hobby of collecting sea shells, and that's only one example. Now then, on with the good work.'

Well, of course, this time I let him get on with it on his own, because I'd had a glance at the ingredients and I could just imagine the state he'd get himself into in his kitchen. But to anyone with a bit of method the recipe is no problem, because I've been making mincemeat for years, and I've only ever dropped five raisins, two dates and a prune, and that was only because someone crept up behind me when I was least expecting it. So try it yourself and see how you get on. Who knows, you may surprise yourself.

Mincemeat

1 lb prunes
1 lb dates
1 lb 8 oz peeled apples
8 oz mixed peel
12 oz brown sugar pieces
12 oz suet
1 lb currants
rind and juice of 2 lemons
2 teaspoons mixed spice
1 teaspoon grated nutmeg
2 tablespoons sherry
pinch salt

Soak the prunes overnight, then drain them, remove the stones, and put them through the mincer with all the other fruits except the currants.

Add the sugar, chopped suet, currants, lemon juice and grated rind, spices, sherry and a pinch of salt. Mix thoroughly. Leave in the basin overnight, and next day put into dry jars.

Tie down and leave in a cool place until required.

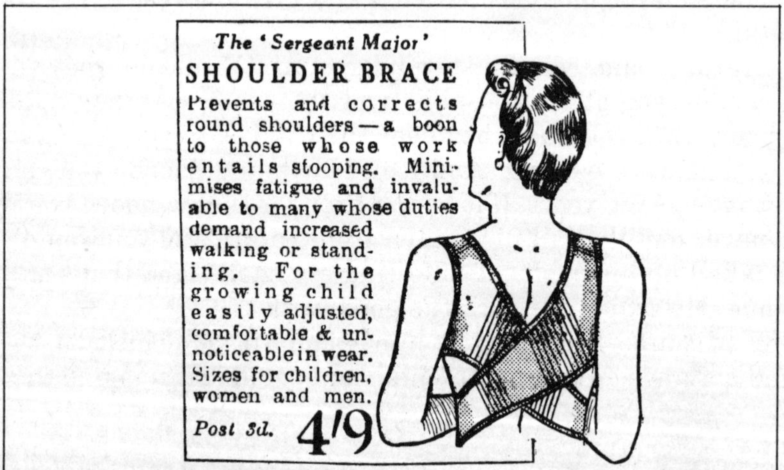

CHRISTMAS

Well, I remember it was just before that Christmas of 1943 that I was out shopping for a couple of blue bags and some cornplasters, when I suddenly bumped into Slack.

'Slack,' I said, 'I haven't seen you since you fell over outside the coal office. How are your legs, and what have you been doing with yourself?'

'Well,' she said, 'I've been going round to Blanche Hackett's every morning with potato peelings and my turnip tops.'

'Fancy,' I said, 'I never realised that Blanche was in such dire straits. She won't make much of a soup with that. I'll take her round a pound of carrots and a parsnip to give it a bit of body.'

'No,' she said, 'Blanche has been fattening up two cockerels for Christmas, and she said she'd give me one provided I helped her to feed it, but last night somebody broke into her shed and stole them, so I don't know what I'm going to do for Christmas dinner now.'

'Slack,' I said, 'put your mind at rest. You shall have your Christmas dinner with me this year, and don't forget to bring your draughts. Yes, I'm sure I can come up with something you'll enjoy. It may not be a banquet, but it will be tasty. And don't breathe a word, but I hear a whisper that Everard has been promised a box of chocolates by a friend, so we should be alright if we talk to him nicely.'

Well, that Christmas morning I was as busy as a bee, and I'd prepared the meal in good time to join everyone for our usual lunchtime drink. Then at two o'clock after we'd had our final drink in the Cock and Trumpet, toasted absent friends and sung a rousing 'Land of Hope and Glory', Slack and I made our way back to my place.

Well, within half an hour we were sitting down at the table with our funny hats on, tucking into one of my favourite dishes, mock duck. Not that Slack twigged, because she'd been at the apricot brandy, and I'm sure if I'd told her it was Mongolian turkey she would have believed me, but she did enjoy it; she even dipped her bread in it!

Mock Duck with Stuffed Onions

6 oz stewing veal
1 lb 8 oz fairly sweet apples
seasoning
stock or gravy
4 large onions
1 teacup breadcrumbs
1 teaspoon chopped parsley
1 dessertspoon chopped sage
a little dripping

Wipe the meat and cut into small pieces. Grease a pie dish or casserole, and place in it layers of meat and sliced apple.

Season, and then half fill the dish with stock or gravy. Cover the dish with greased paper and bake in a moderate oven until the meat is tender, then serve with the stuffed onions.

For the stuffed onions:

Peel the onions, and boil until nearly cooked. Drain thoroughly, and remove and retain the centre from each one.

Chop the removed portions finely, and mix with the breadcrumbs, parsley, sage and seasoning.

Blend with a little dripping, stuff the onions with the mixture, and bake for 15–20 minutes.

Christmas 1943 was when Slack suddenly developed a taste for apricot brandy, and between Christmas and the New Year she'd drink nothing else. Not a lot all at once, but a little taste here and a little taste there, and I think she had one of her best Christmases ever. Now I'm not sure if she was still under the influence, but once again she put pen to paper and wrote the following on New Year's Eve in the Cock and Trumpet. It was called, 'Let's Have an Apricot Brandy'. What else?

Let's Have an Apricot Brandy

Let's have an apricot brandy,
Let's ring out the bells of good cheer,
Let's have an apricot brandy,
As we see in another New Year.

It can't be much worse than the last one,
And I think everyone will agree,
That the best things were Churchill and ITMA
And Ramsbottom and Enoch and Me.

But now we are winning the battle,
We are gradually turning the tide,
And I think we've got Hitler worried,
And he's in for a long bumpy ride.

So, let's have an apricot brandy,
As we wait for the chimes of Big Ben,
In the snug of the old Cock and Trumpet,
And it's time that I put down my pen.

FLORRIE FINCH

Well, in that January of 1944 I went away on tour again, this time with a show called *Tickle your Aunt with a Feather*. It was a very long tour that took us all over the country, and was I worn out! In fact, sometimes I hardly had the strength to dip my buttered osborne into my late-night cocoa. But then I thought, 'help is on the way', because next week is the very last week of the show, and I shall have the pleasure of staying once more with Florrie Finch, one of the finest landladies I've ever had the pleasure to empty tealeaves for.

Yes, Florrie was one of the best, and I remember knocking on her door that cold Sunday afternoon and there she was, the same old Flo, standing there in her kimono and unlaced tennis shoes – her feet used to swell something terrible.

'Flo,' I said, 'how lovely to see you. I haven't seen you since you had that attack of fish poisoning. How are you? Your face has gone down nicely.'

'Lawrence,' she said, 'that must be all of seven years ago, because since then I've had knocker's elbow, dropsy, all my teeth out and two chimney pots blow off.'

'Flo,' I said, 'you'd never know by looking at you. Tell me, is my old room available?'

'Yes,' she said. 'It hasn't been let out since the last time you were here. In fact that glass slipper's still on top of the wardrobe, and there's still that crushed rose under the pillow.'

'Flo,' I said, 'what memories! That was the time when I was in *Cinderella*. What happened to the pumpkin?'

'Well,' she said, 'it shrivelled up to the size of an orange so I threw it out.'

'What a pity,' I said. 'If you'd had two of them you could have made yourself a pair of maracas. Tell me, who else is staying here this week?

'Well,' she said, 'there's two lady acrobats who are performing at the Workman's Hall all the week. They're as tough as old boots, but nice with it. Then there's a Mr Tidmarsh. He's not a theatrical, but he's been staying here with his ferret, and then there's you.'

'Flo,' I said, 'that's not many compared with the old days. I can remember a time when you used to take in the whole cast of *The Fleet's in Port Again* and still have room to sling the odd hammock.'

'Yes,' she said, 'but I wouldn't want all that these days because of the air raids. You see, I haven't got the facilities. Which reminds me, it might be a good idea if you were to sleep with your socks on. Not that we get many raids these days, but you never know.'

Well, I should have known, shouldn't I? Because that very same night I was lying awake thinking, 'I wonder how I shall feel when the Vicar pulls his bell again', when all of a sudden the sirens went!

I was out on the landing like a flash, and there was Flo in her donkey jacket, carrying her miner's lamp, and ushering us all downstairs. 'Come along,' she said. 'You all know where to go.'

'Flo,' I said, 'hold hard, I shan't be a moment, I've forgotten my fleece body-warmer, I shall need it in the shelter, it'll be cold out there.'

'No, it won't,' she said, 'because we haven't got one, but don't worry, we'll be as snug as a bug under the stairs.'

'Flo,' I said, 'you don't mean the cupboard under the stairs where you used to grow your mushrooms! We'll never all get in there!'

'Yes, we will,' she said determinedly. 'It's just a matter of a little twist here and a little turn there, and it's amazing how we'll all fit in.'

How we all managed to get under those stairs I shall never know! Especially as the first thing that happened was that Flo's lamp went out. And, of course, after that it was a case of feel your way.

For the first half-hour someone was sitting on my hands, then somebody did a half circle and finished up sitting on my head, then I spent a further hour sandwiched between the two lady acrobats, and one of those was doing a handstand!

Then somehow we all seemed to find our niche, and I remember sitting there in the dark counting my fingers, when suddenly I felt something making its way up my pyjama leg.

'Heavens!' I cried, 'There's something furry on my fetlock.'

Then a man's voice said, 'I'm sorry about that, it must be my ferret, he's a bit confused.'

'Yes,' I said, 'I can tell. He's going up my other pyjama leg now, and you know what they say about third time lucky.'

Well, how I survived that night I shall never know, and it took me the rest of the week to get my balance back. And what's worse, I had to spend every afternoon with my leg up. But Flo was like an angel, and I only had to tap on the bedroom floor with my stick, and she was there in a flash with a fresh poultice and something to nibble.

But the week finally came to an end, and I remember that when I got home again it was just after D Day, the sixth of June.

Well, as you would have expected, the first person to call on me was Slack. Yes, there she was with a gift of elderberry wine and one of her Cumberland cakes.

'Slack,' I said, 'what a splendid gesture! How have you been all these months?'

'Don't ask me!' she said. 'What with all those doodley bugs that keep coming over, I've been in and out of that shelter like a jack-in-the-box. No wonder my nerves are bad, they put the wind right up my sails.'

'Slack,' I said, 'calm yourself, they'll soon be a thing of the past now that we've landed over there, and it won't be long before you'll be able to climb back into your feather bed and lie there like the Queen of Sheba. And when this war is over, you'll be able to sit up all night eating grapes if you want, just like Mae Murray did in the film *She Dared to Love*. Now then, take off your boots and relax, because I have a little something in my holdall that will get your tastebuds jumping, and take your mind off the war. They were made for me by my last landlady when I left, they're called Coconut Pyramids. Here, get your chops around these.'

Well, of course, Slack wasn't born yesterday, and she knew when she was on to a good thing, so of course she stayed until they were all eaten – I think I had two and she had the rest. Mind you, I never mentioned it to Everard, because I didn't want to go through all the drama about the last strawberry again, so here is the recipe on the quiet, and not a word.

Coconut Pyramids

2 eggs
pinch salt
8 oz desiccated coconut
3 level tablespoons caster sugar

Separate the whites of the eggs from the yolks, and whip the whites with a pinch of salt until they make a stiff froth. Add the coconut and sugar little by little, and beat all the time.

When the mixture has been well beaten together, take a spoonful at a time, and form it into little pyramids on a baking sheet.

Bake in a moderate oven until set and golden brown.

The 'Friend in Hand' public house during alterations.

RONALD COLMAN

Yes, those Coconut Pyramids certainly provided a welcome touch of rare luxury in those days, because everything was still very scarce, and in fact the good old standby was still a good nourishing stew. And nobody could make a more nourishing stew than Slack. I remember as the weather got colder, so the waft of her stews got stronger, and I remember how sometimes there would be three or four people standing by her front gate just sniffing. And Slack always gave a name to her stews. There was wash-day stew, half-day closing stew, thank goodness it's Friday stew and she always kept something special for Sunday.

I remember going round there one Sunday morning, and she insisted that I stayed to lunch as she had made something a bit special.

It was called Irish stew, à la Ronald Colman. Well, I don't know what Ronald Colman had to do with it, I didn't even know he was Irish! But I suppose in a way it was a tribute to her favourite film star. She was always going on about the part he played as an army officer who suffered from shell-shock and lost his memory. And I think the film must have affected her, because she could never remember the name of it. But I think *Lost Horizon* moved her the most, especially at the end when the woman aged a hundred years in about three minutes. And I always remember that bit, because a similar thing happened to Brenda Alcock's mother when the Americans went home in 1946, but that's another story.

Anyway, here is Slack's recipe. Make of it what you will.

Irish Stew, à la Ronald Colman

1 lb neck or scraps mutton
2 lb 8 oz potatoes
$2\frac{1}{2}$ onions
seasoning
$\frac{3}{4}$ pint water

Wipe the meat and cut it into neat pieces. Prepare the potatoes and onions and slice thickly.

Grease a casserole dish and place the meat, potatoes and onions in alternate layers, seasoning each layer.

Pour in the water, put your lid on, and cook in a moderate oven for around $2\frac{1}{2}$ hours.

Well, it was a treat, and I remember saying to Slack, 'Slack, Ronald Colman could have done with some of your stew when he was stuck in that cell in *The Prisoner of Zenda*. If he'd had some of that inside him he would have been able to knock his way through that wall in no time, and then make the hole bigger.'

'Yes,' she said, 'and I always felt sorry for *The Man in the Iron Mask*. Even if they'd offered him stew he wouldn't have been able to manage it, unless they'd let him suck it up with a straw. In fact, I don't know how on earth he did manage all those years.'

'Yes,' I said, 'I've often wondered about that, because if my memory serves me right, he looked fatter when he came out of that cell than when he went in!'

'You're right,' said Slack, 'and when you think of all the things that have happened in the past we've got a lot to be thankful for, because even with a war on we manage to get by somehow. Although I must admit that I do tend to dream of food every so often. In fact, only the other night I dreamt that I was at a banquet with Henry the Eighth, and there he was throwing all those chicken legs over his shoulder, and there I was on my hands and knees picking them up and putting them in my handbag. And I was just about to stick my fork into a nice leg of lamb, when the dog next door knocked the lid off the dustbin and I woke up, so I missed the best bits.'

'You've still got the best bits to come, Slack,' I said. 'You just wait until this war's over, you'll have everything you want and more.'

'I hope so,' she said, 'and I for one can't wait. But meantime it's a case of heads down and grin and bear it.'

And how true that was.

Just a few of the gatecrashers at Brenda Alcock's birthday party on 5 November 1944, when she stood on the kitchen table singing 'Daddy Wouldn't Buy Me a Bow-wow' wearing nothing but a small Union Jack and two Catherine wheels.

STERILISED STAN

Yes, that was the spirit of the times, grin and bear it. I remember saying to Sterilised Stan, 'Stan, how is it that you always manage to whistle on your rounds, even on the coldest morning?'

'Well, if I don't whistle,' he replied, 'my lips freeze together. I'm alright when I get to Doris Witherspoon's because she usually offers me something hot, and in return I try to do something for her lumbago. Then, later on I pop into Vera Titsall's where I have a bowl of soup, a quick prayer, my legs massaged, and a chance to glance at the *Exchange and Mart.*'

'Stan,' I said, 'you certainly lead an interesting life, and you must have made many friends over the years. I know Slack Alice always speaks well of you, she says you're the "top of the milk", and she hates it if she sees someone who hasn't washed their bottles. Yes, I envy you being able to give so many people what they want so early in the morning. Keep up the good work, and give this stick of barley sugar to your horse, he'll think it's his birthday.'

It was people like Stan that kept this country going, out in all weathers, never without a cheery word, and always the first to apologise if he happened to give you the wrong change. And even at Christmas he always seemed a bit embarrassed if you forced a gift of money upon him. That's why one Christmas I thought I would give him something different, a recipe I made up for him myself, called milk float pudding. Yes, he was so overcome, he just took it from me and walked slowly away, but I knew what he was thinking, and that made it all worth while.

Milk Float Pudding

2 level tablespoons grain rice
$\frac{1}{2}$ pint hot water
1 glass milk
1 tablespoon sugar
knob margarine

Put the rice into a pie dish, then add the hot water, and bake in a moderate oven for about 30 minutes, or until the water has been absorbed.

Then add the glass of milk, the sugar and margarine, and bake for a further $1\frac{1}{2}$ hours.

I often wonder if he tried it, but he never mentioned it, and I didn't like to ask.

The man with the confused ferret that nearly nipped me in the bud.

DIP YOUR WICK FOR BRITAIN

Those milk puddings were certainly what everyone needed, because that October of 1944 was a real chiller, and every time someone knocked on my knocker, it was either to borrow some coal or my spare hot-water bottle.

Even the Vicar knocked one day, and he looked as if they'd just brought him home from the Antarctic. 'Vicar,' I said, 'I'm just about to sit down and have a hot muffin, why don't you join me? Pray, what brings you out on a cold day like this?'

'Well,' he said, 'I was wondering if you could possibly lend me a candle?'

'Vicar,' I said, 'I haven't seen a candle for the last three weeks. In fact, I was thinking of coming over and asking you for one, as one of yours would see me through the winter. Don't tell me you've run out of the big ones?'

'Yes,' he said, 'and there seems to be a terrible shortage, I can't get hold of any for love nor money, and even the Archdeacon's stopped answering his doorbell now.'

'That's mean,' I said, 'it's the same with Everard, and I'm sure he's got some hidden away. But Vicar,' I said, 'if you pop around and see Slack she may be able to lend you a night-light.'

'No,' he said, 'I've already called on her, and she was searching her drawers for stumps, and when I think of all the candle-ends I've thrown away, I'd be grateful now for just a couple of inches.'

'Vicar,' I said, 'you're not alone! And I'm sure that Slack feels the same way as well.'

Well, of course, we didn't have to wait long to find out, because the next minute there she was knocking on the door. 'Slack,' I said, 'don't ask! We're all in the same boat.' But, to give her her due, she went out the very next day, bought herself a book on candlemaking, and then sat down and dashed off this poem.

Dip Your Wick for Britain

If you're running out of candles,
Then here's a very simple tip,
Buy a book on candlemaking,
Or 'Easy Ways to Dip your Wick'.

Ask your friends to search their houses,
From the attic to the ground,
For those little bits of candles,
It's surprising where they're found.

When you've got your ends together,
And you've bought a length of wick,
Read the stage-by-stage instructions,
You can make them thin or thick.

So dip you wick to help Great Britain,
And you will be a guiding light,
You know, they say a well-made candle,
Should see you through the darkest night.

SNUG
COCK
VE DAY
PUBLIC BAR

Well, Slack rummaged around all her friends, and she was given so many candle-ends that during that November she was able to turn out some weird and wonderful candles. I remember she made a lovely one for the Vicar, it stood three feet tall and was all the colours of the rainbow. In fact, the Vicar was so taken with it that he couldn't bring himself to light it until Christmas Eve, and even then he blew it out after five minutes. And there was a terrible row on Boxing Day when the Archdeacon called around and tried to commandeer it.

But of course, nerves were getting frayed during that last Christmas of the war, and I even noticed a change in Everard. In fact, he didn't join us at all on Christmas Day, not even for a traditional glass of sherry at the Happy Bullock; he didn't even show his face in the Cock and Trumpet for the loyal toast.

I remember seeing him a few days later as he was putting out his milk bottles, and trying not to catch my eye. I went straight up to him and said, 'Everard, this is the first Christmas I can remember you haven't sent me a Christmas card, and not only that, but you couldn't even bring yourself to invite me in to pull your crackers. I know you always keep yourself to yourself during Lent, but Christmas is supposed to be a time of good cheer. If it hadn't been for Slack inviting me in for Christmas tea, I would have spent most of the day sitting there on my own looking at the four walls, and I'd already turned down an invitation to go to a pint, pie and pickle party at Vera Titsall's and I was dying to see her new stair carpet. Anyway. let's hope that you have a better New Year, and hold out the hand of welcome a bit more. The way you are now, if you smiled your face would crack.'

Anyway, he said nothing so I left him with his thoughts, and sure enough, a couple of days later, there he was standing at my front door.

'Lawrence,' he said, 'I'm ever so sorry about Christmas, but I had a lot of thinking to do. And at last I've made up my mind about my future. From now on, I'm going to devote my life to helping others.'

'Everard,' I said, 'in that case, all is forgiven, because that's just what this world will be needing when this war is over. I know for a fact that Slack won't adjust easily, because these last fives years have been a turning point in her life. How can she settle down to a normal way of life after firewatching on the roof of the Gem, becoming a dab hand with a stirrup pump, and spending hours in her air-raid shelter making candles. Life will seem mundane after all that. And think of Maud; when she's stitched her last parachute, given her last concert in the works' canteen, and her gentleman friend has given his last plunk on his banjo, it won't be easy for them either. And I even feel sorry for Brenda Alcock in a way, because when the Americans go home, she'll be just like her mother – all she'll have is her memories and a wardrobe full of chewing gum.'

But of course, all that was in the future. And a few months later when we had our VE Day celebrations in the Cock and Trumpet, people's thoughts were just for that moment and not for the past or even the future. I remember, as we all raised our glasses, I looked at Slack and thought, 'yes, we've come a long way since that first day when we finished up under the bed.' And as I looked around at all the other faces, I thought to myself, 'yes, here's a toast to all the Slack Alices, the Apricot Lils, the Veras, Mauds, Winns, Cissies, Faiths, Adas, and all the others who did their bit.'

And when the landlord eventually shouted 'Time please', I knew there was something that I would miss now there was no blackout. And that was the landlord shouting out everytime someone came in 'Shut that door!!'

Isn't it funny how some things stick in the mind?

Conversion Tables

OVEN TEMPERATURES

Mark 1	275°F	140°C	slow
2	300°F	150°C	
3	325°F	170°C	
4	350°F	180°C	moderate
5	375°F	190°C	
6	400°F	200°C	hot
7	425°F	220°C	
8	450°F	230°C	

WEIGHTS

1 oz	25 g
2 oz	50 g
4 oz	110 g
8 oz	225 g
12 oz	350 g
1 lb	450 g

VOLUME

¼ pt	150 ml
½ pt	275 ml
¾ pt	425 ml
1 pt	570 ml

All these are approximate conversions, which have been rounded either up or down